M000076754

His
Christmas
Presence

GREG LAURIE

His Christmas Presence

ISBN: 0-9777103-8-6
Published by: Allen David Publishers—Dana Point, California
Coordination: FM Management, Ltd.
Cover design by Chris Laurie
Designed by Highgate Cross + Cathey
Printed in Canada

Contents

ONE

Christmas,
Lost and Found

Children's toys today have become unbelievably more complex and elaborate than the toys of previous generations.

Back in 1960, I remember asking—begging—for a "Mr. Machine" for Christmas. At that time, this was a toy on the very edge of technological sophistication. And I was wildly excited to discover that I actually had it waiting for me that year under the tree.

As I remember, it didn't plug in and didn't have any batteries. By winding a large metal key on Mr. Machine's back, however, he would roll forward, legs and arms moving, bell ringing, and mouth opening and "squawking." You could rotate a little wheel behind the toy to make it run in a circle or curve instead of moving in a straight line.

And that was about it.

I remember thinking that it looked so cool and futuristic, and I felt pretty happy about it until my buddy came over with his new toy.

I had never seen anything like it. It was a little battery-operated plastic scuba diver, outfitted with dual tanks just like Lloyd Bridges on the old *Sea Hunt* TV series.

When you turned it on, the legs kicked. You could put it in your bathtub or wading pool and it would sink to the bottom with bubbles coming out the top.

It was absolutely the edgiest technology I had ever seen. And suddenly I wasn't so happy with my Mr. Machine. I wanted a plastic scuba diver, too.

The funny thing is that as you get older, things really don't change much. What's that old saying? "The only difference between men and boys is the price of their toys." And that's why Christmas is such a letdown for so many people—children and otherwise—because there is such a buildup surrounding the giving and getting of presents.

Here's the basic problem: No matter what you receive, no matter how high the price tag or elaborate the technology, "things" will always disappoint you. If that's what Christmas is all about to you, the holiday will always be a synonym for disappointment.

That's why all of the people out there who work so tirelessly to take Jesus Christ out of Christmas will receive exactly what they want: a meaningless holiday with an emphasis on material possessions and acquiring stuff.

If, however, you want to have the merriest Christmas of all, if you want to experience Christmas the way it was meant to be experienced, you need to understand and embrace the essential message of the season.

Which is simply this: *Immanuel.* God is with us.

THE "ONLY FORGOTTEN SON"

When we think about the reasons for giving Christmas presents to one another, we remember the gifts that the Wise Men brought to the child Jesus. But those weren't the first Christmas gifts. The first gift was God sending His Son into space and time to save us from our sins.

For unto us a Child is born, Unto us a Son is given. (Isaiah 9:6)

For God so loved the world that He gave His only begotten Son, that whoever believes in Him should not perish but have everlasting life. (John 3:16)

My friend Bob Coy, pastor of Calvary Chapel Fort Lauderdale, has a little boy named Christian. One night when he and Christian knelt for prayer by the little boy's bedside, Christian prayed, "And God, thank you for sending your only forgotten Son." It was a mistake. He meant to say, "Your only begotten Son." It makes for a cute story, but there's some truth in what the little boy prayed. For many believers, even at Christmas, Jesus Christ has become God's only forgotten Son.

Let me illustrate. Let's say it is your fortieth birthday, and a large party is given to celebrate that milestone. All of your friends come to the party. There are presents in abundance and a huge cake with fancy writing in the frosting. Your friends get so into the occasion that they actually go out and record songs about you that repeat your name over and over.

So there it is. A big party. Lots of excitement and hoopla. But somehow in all this commotion, no one remembered to invite you, the guest of honor, to your own party!

You assume that it was just an oversight, and you decide to show up at the party anyway, sure that once you arrive the guests will all welcome you with open arms. You arrive at the house, where you see your name emblazoned in lights and you can hear your name being sung in song after song. But nobody responds to your knock at the door, and the door is locked. The music is so loud they can't hear you, and the people are so busy they don't see you. Finally, you shrug your shoulders, walk away from your own party, and drive home.

This is a picture of Christmas for many of us today. We string our lights, we decorate our tree, and we run around buying gifts for those we love (and more gifts for those we don't love) because we feel pressured to do so. We go to countless events and run around like crazy people. But then we have to ask ourselves the question: Has God's only begotten Son become God's only forgotten Son? Have we lost God at Christmas? Is that possible?

Yes, it certainly is, and many of us have experienced such a loss.

Thinking about this "only forgotten Son" reminds me of an incident that the Gospel writer Luke gives us from the boyhood of Jesus.

WHERE IS JESUS?

Joseph, Mary, and Jesus had traveled to Jerusalem for the annual Passover celebration. After spending several days among the thousands of Jews thronging the capital, they packed up and headed for home. Back in those days the men would travel after the women. The women would go on ahead, and the men would follow along behind. So Joseph no doubt assumed that young Jesus was traveling with Mary, and Mary assumed that He was with Joseph.

When they had gone a day's journey down the road, however, they discovered to their shock and dismay that Jesus was absent. He hadn't been with the women or with the men. No one had seen Him.

They had forgotten Jesus!

In all the hubbub of a huge religious celebration, they had forgotten the One whom the Passover was all about. They went back, and eventually found Him in the Temple, "sitting in the midst of the teachers, both listening to them and asking them questions."[1] When Joseph and Mary tried to correct Him, He said, "Did you not know that I must be about My Father's business?"[2]

To me, this story is a picture of today's Christmas celebrations. We get caught up in all the noise and activities and confusion, and forget the One we claim to be honoring. He gets left behind somewhere in the crowd.

Don't lose God this Christmas. Don't forget about Jesus in all the parties and celebrations—and even church services. Find those quiet moments in quiet places where you can draw near to Him, speak to Him, and hear His voice.

The Real Gift of Christmas

The real gift of Christmas isn't something we put on a wish list or under the tree. I'm not talking about Christmas presents here, but rather Christmas presence. His presence.

The presence of God in our lives. Immanuel, God with us.

It boggles the mind to think how God could have been a baby. I think of my newborn grandchild, Stella. She needs constant care. She needs to be nursed and changed and talked to and cared for. And when I think of Almighty God, the Creator of the universe, as a tiny, helpless little baby, it fills me with wonder.

C. H. Spurgeon, the great British preacher, put it this way: "Infinite yet an infant, eternal yet born of a woman, supporting a universe yet needing to be carried in a mother's arms. Heir of all things and yet the carpenter's son."

It can all be summed up beautifully in 2 Corinthians 8:9, where Paul writes, "For you know the grace of our Lord Jesus Christ, that though He was rich, yet for your sakes He became poor, that you through His poverty might become rich."

The promise of Christmas is so tantalizing, so appealing. It promises fulfillment and cheer and brotherly love. And sometimes it delivers. We hear those familiar songs that we remember from our childhood and it gives us a good feeling. But then there is the reality when you go to the mall and people are literally fighting over that one empty parking space. Then you get those gifts under the tree, and maybe you didn't receive what you were hoping for. You left hints for your parents. You left detailed maps to the store. But somehow they missed it, got you something else, and you're disappointed.

Christmas promises so much, but it just can't deliver. It just can't be what you hope it will be, because at best it is a promise of something else—a promise nothing on this earth can fulfill or satisfy.

C. S. Lewis put it this way. "All the things that ever deeply possessed your soul have been but hints of heaven. Tantalizing glimpses. Promises never quite fulfilled. Echoes that died away just as they caught your ear... If I find in myself a desire which no experience in this world can satisfy, the most probable explanation is that I was made for another world. Earthly pleasures were never meant to satisfy. But to arouse, to suggest the real thing."[3]

The "real thing" Lewis was speaking of is heaven. When it's all said and done, when the food has been consumed, the parties are over, and the tree goes out on the curb for the garbage truck, it's not about Christmas presents. It is about His Christmas presence in our life. Christmas is not about giving a gift as much as it is about receiving a gift. The Bible says, "For the wages of sin is death, but the free gift of God is eternal life through Christ Jesus our Lord."[4] It goes on to say, "Thanks be to God for His indescribable gift!"[5]

When someone offers you a gift, all you need to do is take it and open it. His wonderful presence can be yours right now, and forever.

I remember reading an article in the newspaper about a man who had a nativity scene set up on his front yard. You know the typical scene. Mary and Joseph. The little baby Jesus. A few sheep thrown in. All of these figures had little lights in them.

Then one night some vandals came along and stole his little plastic baby Jesus with a ten-watt bulb inside. This guy got really stressed out about it. The local newspaper interviewed him, and in the article he pleaded with the robber to "please bring Jesus back to me."

I read that and thought, "You know what, buddy? Maybe you need to get a life. We're talking a plastic replica here." But to him that was really important.

In a broad sense, you might say that this man was looking for Jesus. Unfortunately, his Jesus was a plastic baby with a light bulb inside. But at least he thought enough of Jesus to miss the plastic replica! Many other people this time of year are working feverishly to remove any remembrance of Jesus from public view.

These are generally the same people who have tried to remove the "one nation under God" phrase from our pledge of allegiance, labored tirelessly to keep prayer out of our schools, gone to court to keep anyone from seeing the Ten Commandments posted in public view, and have generally done everything they could to remove the name of Jesus Christ—or even the word "Christmas"—from their no-name holiday celebrations.

In Portland, Maine, a site manager for that city's housing authority recently attempted to clarify a new policy banning all religious celebrations or decorations. It mandated that "There shall be no angels, crosses, stars of David or any other icons of religion displayed on the walls, floors, ceilings, etc. of your apartment buildings except within your own apartment." The dictum went on to decree that anything hanging on the inside of the resident's door was permissible, but nothing whatsoever was allowed on the outside, exposed to the hallway, because "it might offend someone."

Or how about the grade school principal in Sacramento, California, who strictly warned his teachers against using the word "Christmas" on any written materials within their classrooms.

In case you haven't noticed, the new politically correct greeting this time of the year is no longer "Merry Christmas," but the more generic, (insipid) "happy holidays."

I refuse to say happy holidays. My recommendation? Say "Merry Christmas" to people—cheerfully, distinctly, politely, and without shame! Or when you receive one of those wimpy "happy holidays" greetings, smile your brightest smile and say, "Why thank you! And God bless you," or "Jesus loves you." We who belong to Jesus ought to have no shame in declaring His name or His love. We own Him in public, just as He owns us.

The attempt to remove every vestige of Christmas, however, has gone to almost-unbelievable lengths. Now even the humble snowflake has been deemed offensive. In Saratoga Springs, New York, third graders at Division Street Elementary School saw their Christmas project confiscated by an indignant principal. Entering their classroom, he was struck with horror when he saw the boys and girls adorning an oversized Christmas ornament with colored photos of snowflakes. He quickly removed the offending item from sight, and there is no word as to whether the teacher was allowed to keep her job. (She probably had to attend sensitivity training.)

Others have banned poinsettias for alleged "religious connotations."

All of this seems incredibly sad to me. But when you think about it, there's something even more sad than that. There are sincere believers in the Lord Jesus Christ who will lose sight of Him this year during the very season set apart to honor His entry into our world.

MISSING PERSON

Did you ever feel as though you somehow lost God from your life? One day as you were going about your affairs, you suddenly realized that something was missing. And that's when it dawned on you that you hadn't given a single thought to God all day… or maybe for several days. That connection with heaven you had always enjoyed seemed distant at best. It was almost as though He were gone.

I heard the story of a little boy who wandered into a local church. Wide-eyed, he saw all the candles lit for a time of prayer. Misunderstanding the meaning of those symbols, he proceeded to blow out all of the candles and sing "Happy Birthday" to Jesus.

The minister, who observed all this, was incensed. When the boy walked out the doors, the priest followed him home. After the little guy went into his house, the minister knocked on the door, and the boy's mother answered.

"Yes, Reverend, what can I do for you?"

He replied, "Ma'am, I want to speak with your son. He has no respect for God whatsoever."

With a sigh, she said, "Okay, Father, come on in. I'll get him."

The little boy walked slowly down the stairs from his room, coming to stand in front of the stern-faced man of the cloth.

"I have a question for you, son," he said. "Where is God?"

The boy didn't know what to say.

Again the minister leaned forward, and said, "Little boy, I asked you a question. Where is God?" At this, the boy's eyes went wide as saucers and he started to tremble. When the minister asked him one more time, the little boy bolted out of the room, ran upstairs, and slammed the door of his bedroom behind him.

His mother ran to his room and said, "Honey, what's wrong?"

"Mommy," her son said in a frightened voice, "they have lost God at that church, and they think I took Him!"

We can lose God in the holiday season. But here is something to consider. If you feel far from God, guess who moved? God hasn't gone anywhere. . . but maybe you have. And in the busyness of the season and in the so-called celebration of the birth of Christ we can forget all about Him.

You know how it is. . . On Wednesday there's a "white elephant" party at the office. Then on Thursday, there's that special Christmas movie you wanted to see with the family. And the weekend? Yikes! You haven't sent Christmas cards yet. . . and there's so much shopping. . . how will you ever get it all done?

And somewhere in it all, we lose track of our Lord.

Maybe there was a point in your life when you walked closely with the Lord, but in recent days it seems like you've lost sight of Him.

A Lost Love

I'm reminded of the words of Jesus to the church of Ephesus in Revelation 2, when He says,

> *"I know your deeds, your hard work and your perseverance. I know that you cannot tolerate wicked men, that you have tested those who claim to be apostles but are not, and have found them false. You have persevered and have endured hardships for my name, and have not grown weary.*
>
> *"Yet I hold this against you: You have forsaken your first love. Remember the height from which you have fallen! Repent and do the things you did at first. If you do not repent, I will come to you and remove your lampstand from its place."*[6]

To read this account, it sounds as though the First Church of Ephesus was a busy, active, productive church. They wouldn't tolerate false teaching, and they seemed to have all their doctrinal ducks in a row. But somehow in all that activity, work, and study, they had lost sight of Jesus.

And the Lord Himself has to say to them, "You have left your first love."

Work had taken the place of worship. Perspiration had taken the place of inspiration. So the Great Physician, our Lord Himself, writes them a prescription for renewal

or revival. Remember from where you have fallen. Repent
and do the first works quickly. I sum it up like this: There
are three R's of getting right with God—Remember,
Repent, Repeat.

"Get Back"

So maybe there was a time when you were closer to God,
but for whatever reason, you're not in that place anymore.
You can remember what it was like. You read one of your
old journals and it seems to just overflow with love for
Jesus. But now there's a distance.

What do you do? In the immortal words of Saint Paul,
Saint John, Saint George, and Saint Ringo, "Get back, get
back, get back to where you once belonged." In other words,
remember where you were, and go back to that place.

Do you remember the way it was when you first came to
Jesus Christ? Do you remember the passion, the excitement?

I saw a movie recently that included the testimonies of
a group of young surfers who had all come to Christ. And
it was so refreshing to hear the stories of these young men
who had come out of a life of partying and drugs and all
that other stuff that young kids get themselves into. One
of them came to Christ and started telling all his friends
about the Lord. One by one, this whole group of friends
gave their lives to Christ, and now they're all serving Him.

Some of these guys were very successful in their sport,
and had lots of honors and accolades thrown their way.
They were making money and acquiring some fame. But
at the same time, all of them admitted to an emptiness in
their lives—an emptiness now filled to overflowing by a

relationship with God through Jesus. And they were talking about how thrilling it was to study the Bible and pray together.

I'm reminded of thousands who have come to Christ through the years of our ministry in places all over the world. There's almost always an evidence that something is different, something has changed. There are changed priorities as you seek to know Him better and walk with Him more closely. You look forward to being with other believers at church and at Bible studies and worship times. You're excited about getting alone with God in prayer.

Frankly, if these things don't draw you and excite you, that would tell me there's something spiritually wrong. It would tell me that maybe you need to get back to where you were. . . where you should be. Remember from where you have fallen. Repent and change your direction. And repeat, doing those things you used to do when Jesus was number one in your life.

It's amazing how we can go through a day and never think about Jesus. In many ways we can live like a practical atheist, with no thought of God whatsoever except when we get our food. "Oh yeah. Let's pray. Lord, uh bless this food. Hello. Good-bye."

Have you lost sight of Jesus? As we enter a new year let's make a real effort to remember Him by taking time for the Word of God. And by that I mean carve out time for Bible study. Don't just try to work it into your busy schedule. Change your busy schedule and make time for God's Word.

Let's remember Him by taking time each and every day for prayer—a time to spend in the presence of God, listening to His voice as well as baring your heart to Him and bringing your petitions to Him. Jesus said, "Men always ought to pray and not give up."[7]

Let's remember Him by our involvement in church, with His people. Not just working it in when you can find time, but understanding that there is a priority in gathering with God's people for worship and prayer. Church is not just a place where we take in. It is also a place where we give out. It is a place to use the gifts that God has given to us, seek spiritual accountability, and listen to the advice that others can give to us. It is a place to invest our finances and share in what God is doing.

Remember Him also as you look for opportunities to share your faith with others. The Christmas season is such a natural time to speak about Jesus, and to tell others about this One who has been born and was crucified and has risen again from the dead.

Don't lose Jesus this Christmas.

I read an article awhile ago about a man who got his circuits overloaded during the Christmas season and, before the day was over, ended up in jail.

Here's what happened. After rummaging through some boxes in the garage, he finally found the Christmas lights to put up around his house. Unfortunately, they were wadded up in a giant ball (his wife had packed them up in a hurry the previous Christmas).

Upset with his wife for leaving the lights in such a mess, he grumbled and muttered as he sought to untangle them.

Finally, he managed to get all the cords stretched out and knot-free on his driveway. Just as he had turned to enter the garage for the stepladder, his daughter wheeled into the driveway in her car and ran over all the lights he had just spent forty minutes unraveling.

That's when he lost it. He bellowed at his daughter for not looking before pulling into the driveway. Then he told his wife, "I need to go blow off a little steam." Pulling his .45-caliber pistol out of a drawer, while his family decorated the tree, he went out into his backyard and began firing off shots into the ground.

Someone called the police, as you might expect, and the officers arrested the man for reckless endangerment. He explained to the police that he had been attending some anger management classes, and thought discharging his pistol would help him discharge his anger. Then the police took away his concealed weapons permit and he had something new to be mad about.

In the case of that family, someone might have revised the lyrics of "Chestnuts Roasting on an Open Fire" to "Chestnuts Roasting as He Opens Fire." This is a classic example of a guy who missed the whole point of Christmas. That's the way it can be for many people this time of year.

FALSE EXPECTATIONS

You can make seemingly innumerable trips to the malls. You can hear and sing countless Christmas songs and give gifts to everyone imaginable. Even your dog. That's right,

gifts for dogs are the newest marketing rage. You're supposed to feel guilty because everyone gets something nice
except poor old Fido. Like your dog could even care.

Anyway, people these days are remembering their dogs
at Christmas, but forgetting the One whose birth, life,
death, and resurrection they are supposedly celebrating.
Many of us become so preoccupied this time of year that
we forget about the Lord and about making room for Him
in our lives. In all the clutter of our activity, we can miss
Jesus Christ.

I have read that during this time of the year depression
rates go up dramatically. More people check into hospitals.
Suicide rates go up in the holiday season. More people seek
psychological help.

One fifty-four-year-old woman who was seeking psycho-
therapy during the holidays made this statement: "I get
sad at Christmas. I feel like there's a big gap in what it's
supposed to be about spiritually. I don't feel that I want
to get into this material glut. I think deep down inside
we are all afraid of dying. I think the terrorist attacks
brought that home to us on a very large, horrendous scale."

The truth is, we feel let down and disappointed because
of false expectations as to what Christmas should be.

Some people don't mind taking time off to commemo-
rate the birth of Jesus, but that's the extent of it. He is all
right as long as He stays in that manger as a baby. They
don't like the idea of Jesus growing into a man and telling
them to turn from their sin and dying on a cross for them
and rising again from the dead.

There are many people who say, "I'm okay with God as long as He stays out of my life." They might have a bumper sticker on their car that says, "God is my co-pilot." That's nice. But the fact of the matter is, you shouldn't even be in the cockpit. God doesn't want to be your co-pilot. He wants to be in control of your life.

But that's where people want God. They want Him there in case of emergency, and that's about the extent of their faith. These people wrongly think they make their own luck, that they are the captains of their own ship, the masters of their own destiny.

ESCAPING THE TRAP

Some look down on Christians and say, "You people are a bunch of automatons marching in lockstep. You want to do the will of God. Well, fine. But I want to do the will of me. I'm in control of my own life. I decide what direction I am going to take."

I have news for you. Life doesn't work that way.

People who reject Jesus Christ are not in control of their own lives, nor are they making their own luck. According to the Bible, those outside of Christ are under the control of someone else. And that someone else is known as Satan.

In 2 Timothy 2:26, Paul writes this word to believers: "Be humble when you are trying to teach those who are mixed up concerning the truth. For if you talk meekly and courteously to them they are more likely, with God's help, to turn away from their wrong ideas and believe what is true.

Then they will come to their senses and escape from Satan's trap of slavery to sin which he uses to catch them whenever he likes, and then they can begin doing the will of God."[8]

You don't realize this when you're a nonbeliever. You imagine yourself to be in charge of your own life. You convince yourself that you're calling all the shots. But it's strange. Have you ever noticed how most nonbelievers do the same things? They get caught up into the same miserable lifestyle. And then one day, by God's grace, they wake up and look around and say, "What is this? What am I doing here? How did I get to this place? I hate this life."

That's what happened in Jesus' story of the lost son. This was the young man who took his share of his dad's inheritance, left for Vegas (or something like that), blew all his money, and ended up as a farm laborer feeding pigs in a pigpen. As he was watching the fat hogs grub around in the muck for scraps, he found himself thinking some of those scraps were looking pretty good.

That's when it hit him. The Bible says, "he came to his senses." And then he said, "I will go to my father."[9]

That's what happened to me, too, as a young man. I started looking around at my life and thought, *This stinks. I'm sick of these stupid parties. I'm tired of drinking and drugs. I can't stand all of these cliques, and the way these people live. I've had enough of all the backstabbing and hypocrisy. There has to be something better.*

Those thoughts, that inner restlessness and dissatisfaction, sent me on a quest to find purpose and meaning.

I thought, "Surely there's more to life than this." The adult world that I'd been exposed to certainly wasn't the world where I wanted to live. The empty, unhappy lives of my friends and peers didn't appeal to me either.

So I started looking. My search led me to hearing the gospel and giving my life to Christ. Then I started coming to church, hanging out with God's people, and seeing the reality I had been searching for all along. I found a place where love and brotherhood and joy could be experienced—not because you were high on something, but through a relationship with God.

TRAPPED BY RELIGION

The religious teachers completely missed Jesus.

We'll consider this in more detail later, but Herod called these theological experts in after the Wise Men asked, "Where is He who is born king of the Jews?" They knew the answer all right. It was Bethlehem. They could quote chapter and verse to the evil king. And yet these men—the supposed guardians of spiritual truth in Israel—wouldn't bother to walk a few miles south to Bethlehem to find out if the Messiah of Israel had indeed been born.

At least Herod feared Jesus' authority—and tried to nip it in the bud. The innkeeper could claim busyness and ignorance. But what about these men? They knew better. They knew the Word of God, and yet they did nothing to respond to it. They were indifferent. They were too busy with themselves to be concerned about Jesus. In fact, when His public ministry began, they became His principal adversaries.

For all practical purposes these were the very men responsible for the execution of Jesus Christ. Why? Because He was a threat to their little religious empire. The Bible says that they sent Him up to Pilate out of envy. They envied His authority. They envied the fact that the people loved Him and hung on His every word. They envied the fact that He seemed to have a relationship with God that they lacked.

Addressing this at a later date, Jesus said, "Isaiah was right when he prophesied about you hypocrites; as it is written: 'These people honor me with their lips, but their hearts are far from me. They worship me in vain; their teachings are but rules taught by men.' "[10]

They were looking for a different kind of Messiah. They didn't want a Messiah who would suffer and die on a cross for them. They were looking for someone who would support their religious system and their chosen way of life— someone who would cater to their whims and conform to their wishes. Someone who would keep them in power.

There are many people like this today. They want Jesus, but they want Him on their terms.

They want the kind of Jesus that they can control.

The kind of Jesus who will never challenge them.

The kind of Jesus who won't ask them to change their ways.

They want heaven, but they don't want talk about hell.

They want forgiveness, but they are unwilling to repent.

They want the cross, but they don't want Christ.

I heard a true story about a woman who went into a jewelry store and began looking at various crosses and crucifixes.

After examining them for a while, she said to the jeweler, "Do you have any crosses without this little man on them?" That's how it is for many people today. They want religion, but only according to their own sensibilities. They want truth, but only if it aligns with "their truth."

The fact is, religion can be a deadly trap. When all is said and done, more people will be sent to hell by religion than by all of the wicked and sinful vices this world has to offer.

MAN-MADE RELIGION

I have never had any interest in being a religious person. Religion holds no allure to me. The mystery of religious ritual has no appeal to me whatsoever. But I am very interested in a relationship with God. I am interested in truth. I am interested in knowing right and wrong. I am interested in what happens to me after I die. I am interested in the Bible. I am very interested in what Jesus has to say. But I am not interested at all in religion.

What's the difference, you ask?

All the difference in the world. Religion, with its man-made rules and rituals, can seduce you into thinking that everything is okay between you and the Lord.

For me, religion is like eating a side salad. I really don't like salad. For me, a salad is like practicing for real food. My wife can go to a restaurant and her entrée is salad. That's it. Salad and maybe a paltry cup of soup. I say, "Are you kidding? Is that all you're eating?" For me,

salad is a warm-up. I want real food. If I ate a salad, I'd
be hungry an hour later because it just doesn't satisfy me.
Religion does that. It gives you something to chew on,
something to occupy yourself with, but leaves you empty
and unsatisfied. It never really touches your hunger.

There are other ways that religion can deceive you.
You say, I went to church this morning, gave my confession
to the priest, and received holy communion. Or maybe, I
was baptized or confirmed, and now I can sin up a storm
because I suffered in church for two hours today. I've paid
my dues and earned my Brownie points with God, so now
I can go out and live as I please.

What a warped concept of what faith is all about! If you
believe things like these, you are being deceived by religion.

Sometimes you will talk to someone and say, "You need
Jesus." And they will reply, "Well, I'm a Catholic... or a
Baptist... or a Pentecostal... so I'm okay." That's religious
deception! What really counts isn't the brand name on your
church, it's who lives in your heart. That is what matters.

That's what these religious leaders did. They knew the
Word. They could quote it verbatim. Yet they did nothing
to meet the living Savior.

———————————

On December 17, 1903, brothers Orville and Wilbur
Wright made the very first airplane flight at Kitty Hawk,
North Carolina, on their fifth attempt. With Orville at the
controls, the primitive aircraft got off the ground for twelve
seconds.

It was an epic event... the first time man had ever flown. Wilbur rushed to the telegraph office with a message for his sister, Catherine. The message read: "We have flown for 12 seconds. We will be home for Christmas."

Upon receiving this telegram, Catherine hurried to the newspaper office to speak with the editor. After describing her brothers' flying machine and what they accomplished at Kitty Hawk, she mentioned that Orville and Wilbur would both be home for Christmas if he would like to set up an interview. The editor smiled and said he would be sure to put something in the paper about what the Wright boys were up to.

And so on December 19th, the local newspaper ran the following headline on the sixth page of the newspaper: "WRIGHT BROTHERS HOME FOR CHRISTMAS."

Talk about missing the point. Here was the most important story of the year, indeed of the century—man's first flight—and this editor missed it. It blew right over his head.

That's exactly how Christmas is for many today.

MISSING THE POINT

So many people completely miss the point of Christmas. The truth is, Christmas has been hijacked by secular culture and emptied of its meaning. And there is so much fantasy and myth imposed on this holiday that people have become numb to the real miracle of Christ's birth.

I heard the story of a lady who took her little boy to Sunday school for the first time, where he heard the story of our Lord's birth. It was all new to him; he'd never heard anything like it.

When he got home, he excitedly described it all to his mom.

"Mom," he said, "today I learned about the very first Christmas in Sunday school. There wasn't a Santa Claus back then, but there were these three skinny guys on camels that had to deliver all of the toys. And Rudolph the Red-Nosed Reindeer with his nose so bright wasn't there yet, so they had to have this big spotlight from the sky to guide these three skinny guys around."

That's a pretty good illustration of how our reference point has changed as a culture. Many of our children start with the shallow Christmas myths but don't know anything about the real, historical account that launched everything—the greatest story of all.

In all the madness that accompanies this season, we can actually miss Christmas. You say, "Greg, it's not possible to miss Christmas. My Sunday newspaper weighs in at about 30 pounds because it is stuffed with ads pressuring me to buy stuff. The TV is reminding me. The radio is reminding me. Even when I go on the Internet, there are those obnoxious little pop-up ads that remind me. To tell you the truth, I'm worn out by it all."

I'm reminded of a story I heard about a mother who was running furiously from store to store on Christmas Eve to get those last-minute gifts. Suddenly, she realized she had lot track lost track of her little three-year-old son. In a panic, she retraced her steps and found her little guy with his nose pressed up against a frosty window, gazing at a manger scene.

When he heard his mother shout out his name, he said, "Mommy, Mommy, look! It's the baby Jesus in the hay."

The stressed-out mom grabbed him and jerked him away, saying, "We don't have time for that. Can't you see Mommy is trying to get ready for Christmas?"

That is how it can be. Because of all the clutter of Xmas—and I use that term intentionally—we forget about the Christ of Christmas. So come back to the manger of Bethlehem, and Christmas will come alive to you.

"WHO'S RESPONSIBLE FOR THIS?"

A woman was doing some last-minute Christmas shopping at a crowded mall. She was tired of fighting the crowds and standing in lines and getting all those gifts and so forth. Finally almost done with her shopping, she pushed the elevator button, the door opened, and it was packed with people.

Have you ever had that moment? Everyone looks at you with an expression that says, "Don't come in here."

But you really don't want to wait any longer, because you've already waited a long time. So she wedged her way into the packed elevator.

As they were on their way down, she just couldn't hold her frustrations in any longer. Breaking all the rules of elevator decorum, she suddenly blurted out, "Whoever is responsible for this whole Christmas thing ought to be arrested, strung up, and shot!" A few others nodded in agreement. And then at the back of the elevator came a single voice that said, "Don't worry. They already crucified Him."

Now Jesus is certainly not responsible for the madness of Christmas. He wasn't born that we might shop, He was born to die that we might live. There was no room for Him at the inn. In fact, it seems the only place where there was room for Him was on the cross.

But listen. Often those who are conversant with spiritual truth are in the greatest danger of indifference. If you are in a good, Bible-teaching church, you are blessed with the privilege of hearing the Word of God taught day and in and day out. But there is a danger that comes with that blessing. If you listen to those truths with a wrong heart, with no intention of applying what you've heard, if you're just going through the motions, your heart can actually grow hard to the things of God.

If contact with holy things does not convert or change your heart, it can cause your heart to become jaded and cynical. We can become indifferent or flippant about the tender story of the nativity. We can become jaded to the message of the gospel because we have heard it so many times. As so many through the years have affirmed, familiarity breeds contempt. Don't let that happen to you. Keep a tender and open heart to God. Don't let religion crowd out Jesus. Don't miss Christmas. Make time for Jesus. Make room for Jesus. I love the Christmas hymn "Joy to the World," because one of the lines says, "Let every heart prepare Him room."

Make room for Him this year.

TWO

Hurried, Worried, and Buried

Though I have seated myself in front of the computer to write about Christmas joy, I have to be honest here. Shopping can really stress me out in December. This year especially, it seems like everything ended up costing a whole lot more than I thought it would.

It reminds me of "The Twelve Days of Christmas."

You know that tune, don't you? It's kind of a bizarre song when you think about it. I suppose it's speaking about the extravagance of buying just the right presents for your "true love." But when you total all of those presents up over the twelve days, you'd have to be Bill Gates or Donald Trump to pull it all off.

It starts, of course, with a partridge in a pear tree. (Something that's never been particularly high on my Christmas list.) Then there are two turtle doves, three French hens, four calling birds, five golden rings, six geese a-laying, seven swans a-swimming, and on it goes. Experts put the cost of all 364 items mentioned in the song at $65,264.

By the way... that's up 19 percent from a year ago.

Eight maids a-milking and ten lords a-leaping are about the same price as last year, but the 11 pipers and 12 drummers must belong to a musicians' union, because they are 28 percent more expensive this season than last season.

I don't know about you, but I'm ready to be done with it. Not the celebration of the birth of Jesus, of course, but all of the hoopla of Christmas.

Most of us aren't really sick of Christmas, we're sick of what it has become in our culture. But when we set all the accoutrements and add-ons aside, and just get back into the simple account of our Lord's birth in Scripture, joy springs up like an artesian well. And that's exactly what we need to get back to.

As I see it, here's our main problem: Many of us try to find joy and happiness in Christmas, when we really need to find the joy and happiness in Christ Himself. And that is a very big difference.

When you place your hopes and expectations on a particular celebration or special day on the calendar, you'll find yourself disappointed again and again. But when you place your hopes and expectations on the Lord Himself, He will never, never let you down.

And this hope will not lead to disappointment. For we know how dearly God loves us, because he has given us the Holy Spirit to fill our hearts with his love. (Romans 5:5, NLT)

Let's revisit now that most beautiful of all stories in Luke's second chapter.

THE TIMELESS STORY

And it came to pass in those days that a decree went out from Caesar Augustus that all the world should be registered. This census first took place while Quirinius was governing Syria. So all went to be registered, everyone to his own city. Joseph also went up from. . . Nazareth, into Judea, to the city of David, which is called Bethlehem, because he was of the house and lineage of David, to be registered with Mary, his betrothed wife, who was with child. So it was, that while they were there, the days were completed for her to be delivered. And she brought forth her firstborn Son, and wrapped Him in swaddling cloths, and laid Him in a manger, because there was no room for them in the inn. (Luke 2:1-7)

Dr. Luke, the author of this Gospel, reports the facts in meticulous detail. He begins by giving us specific historical information so we can pinpoint this event in human time.

History tells us that Caesar Augustus was the great-nephew of Julius Caesar. A born in-fighter, he had clawed his way into power by defeating Antony and Cleopatra. Then, through considerable genius and force, he gave the Roman Empire a solidity that lasted for centuries. He was the first Caesar to take on the title of "Augustus," which means "of the gods" or "the holy and revered one."

Luke was a stickler for detail. Although he was not one of the twelve disciples nor—as far as we know—an eye witness of the life and ministry of Jesus, he was the man chosen afterwards by the Holy Spirit to put together an accurate account of what Jesus said and did.

In his first chapter, he wrote: "Having carefully investigated everything from the beginning, I also have decided to write a careful account for you, most honorable Theophilus, so you can be certain of the truth of everything you were taught."[11] Like a trained journalist, this physician interviewed many of the key players in putting together a precise account of Christ's life and work.

Not only was Luke a stickler for detail, he was also a poet. Even translated into English, his writing reflects dignity and beauty, using descriptive language that helps us see it all (two millennia later) in our mind's eye as we read it.

In subsequent years, archaeologists unearthed an inscription dating back to the reign of this Roman ruler. It read: "Augustus Caesar, the savior of the whole world."

That is how this Caesar saw himself. . . which gives Luke 2:11 a whole new dimension of meaning, when the angel says: "Unto you is born this day in the City of David a Savior, which is Christ the Lord."[12] Essentially the angel was saying, "Don't look to the palace of Rome for the Savior of the world. Look to the manger in Bethlehem. Don't look at that self-proclaimed, satin-robed god in Rome, but look at that humble Baby wrapped in swaddling clothes."

When you really consider the incarnation and life of Jesus, it's not a rags-to-riches story, it's a riches-to-rags story.

He gave up everything—the unimaginable splendor of heaven—to serve us and to save us.

On one of Queen Elizabeth's recent visits to the United States, she brought along 5,000 pounds of clothing. (She probably didn't do "carry-on.") Her entourage included two personal valets and her own hairdresser. I read that she even brought her own special leather covers for the toilet seats used by her highness.

That is not traveling light.

Obviously she didn't leave any of the comforts of home. She brought them all with her so she could continue to live in luxury as the head of the royal family.

But look at what Jesus left to come to us. Try to imagine what He left, what He gave up. The Bible says that "though he was God, he did not think of equality with God as something to cling to. Instead, he gave up his divine privileges; he took the humble position of a slave and was born as a human being."[13]

His Story

God moved Caesar Augustus—this little man who was so big in his own eyes—to set forth a decree that everyone should be taxed. Caesar probably congratulated himself on his own good idea to raise the empire's revenue in this way. Caesar thought he was the ultimate king, but in reality, he was just a little pawn on God's chessboard. The actual reason for that tax was to get Mary and Joseph to Bethlehem, where the Messiah was to be born.

The Bible specifically said that the little village of Bethlehem would be the unlikely spot for this momentous event.

But you, Bethlehem Ephrathah,
Though you are little among the thousands of Judah,
Yet out of you shall come forth to Me
The One to be Ruler in Israel,
Whose goings forth are from of old,
From everlasting.
(Micah 5:2)

God moved human events to cause this prophecy to be fulfilled. History is His story. It has been said that history swings on the hinge of the door of a stable in Bethlehem. This was the one moment in all of time—"in the fullness of time," as the Scripture says—when God chose to deliver the greatest of all gifts to His rebellious world. . . the gift of His own Son as Messiah and Savior.

Most of the known world at that time was united under one system of imperial government. Rome had bludgeoned the world into submission, vanquishing all enemies. This forced peace—peace at the point of the sword—became known as "Pax Romana" or "the peace of Rome."

With the absence of war in the civilized world, people were able to devote more time than usual to pursuits such as literature, art, philosophy, and religion. Greek philosophers like Plato led people into pondering the great imponderables about life, destiny, and human character. As never before, people across the world were probing and searching for meaning.

It could have been a priceless opportunity for God's people, the Jews, to hold high the light of the true and living God. For the most part, however, it was an opportunity lost. If seekers turned to the Judaism of that day, they were bound to be disappointed. Instead of finding a vibrant, living faith as in the glory days of David and Solomon, they would instead find an empty shell, weighted down with innumerable rituals, rules, and regulations that the religious leaders themselves couldn't keep, much less the average man or woman.

Even so, there was something in the air. The rabbis spoke of it. The poets wrote of it. Something was stirring. Something was coming.

And it had been a very, very long time coming. Before the angel appeared to Zacharias in the Temple, foretelling the birth of John the Baptist, there had been 400 years of silence from heaven. No prophets proclaiming their visions, no angels delivering messages, no miracles to stir people's hearts.

Nothing.

Everything was quiet.

And then everything changed... forever.

BREAKING THE SILENCE

A mighty angel named Gabriel broke the 400-year silence by appearing in the Temple to the old priest Zacharias, with the promise of a son born to him and his wife, Elizabeth. That son would become the greatest prophet in the history of Israel and a direct herald and forerunner of the Messiah.

Following this event in quick succession, the angel came to Mary with the announcement that she would conceive supernaturally in her womb, and then on to Joseph to confirm the miracle.

Mary was well along in her pregnancy when she and Joseph were compelled to journey to Bethlehem to register with the government and pay their taxes. God was moving human events so she and Joseph would get to Bethlehem before the birth, fulfilling the specific prophecies of Messiah's birth.

Joseph was of the house and lineage of David, Israel's second king. That's why he had to go to Bethlehem, David's old hometown. Fulfilling biblical prophecy was probably the last thing on this couple's mind as they made that difficult trip. Both of them were probably very concerned about getting to Bethlehem and back home again before the baby arrived.

What the tired couple needed when they came into Bethlehem was a nice motel. Or just any motel! As they walked through town, however, all they could see on every hand was an absence of "vacancy" signs. They came to the inn where they had hoped to stay, but there was no room for them and they were turned away.

Presumably it was an innkeeper who delivered this bad news. He could clearly see that Mary was well along in her pregnancy, and that she needed a clean and warm room in case she was to give birth. But he stood at the door of the inn and shook his head. "Sorry," he said, "no room. Nothing available."

Frankly, it's hard for me to imagine a man being that heartless. Call me old-fashioned if you like, but I'm one of those people who believe that when a woman is headed toward a door, a man should open that door for her. I know very well that some women don't appreciate that these days, but I think there are still a lot of women who do. And if I'm seated in a train or a bus and a woman walks in with no place to sit, I give her my seat. It's a matter of common courtesy—especially if she is an older woman. And certainly if she is a pregnant woman. I think we should go out of our way to assist a pregnant woman because of the discomfort that pregnancy brings. I want to make it a little easier for her.

So I have a difficult time with this innkeeper, who turned away an obviously pregnant young woman and her husband. It seems like just simple human kindness would demand that he clear a space for these two, put a roof over them, and prepare for the possibility that she might give birth that night.

In this woman's womb was the creator of the universe in human form. And this guy was too busy to give them the time of day, much less a place of rest and shelter.

And if you were Joseph, with responsibility for this woman and the unborn child, you would find yourself saying, Now what? As it turned out, there was a ramshackle little building—or perhaps a cave—behind the inn that was used as a stable for the animals. With no other options, it was there that Joseph finally sought shelter for the night.

It's easy to vilify a man like this innkeeper and think of him as a wicked man. That could have been the case. But more plausibly, I think he was probably just a very preoccupied and busy man. Occupied with making money, he had all the business he could handle that night and didn't take time to consider "the right thing to do."

It reminds me of our country today, and those who have no time to seek God. You invite people to church and they reply, "Well, we're just too busy right now. We have so much to do."

We say, "Why don't you come to church with us on Christmas?" And we hear replies like, "That's a nice idea, but... we're going to a play... this movie just opened... we have to do a bit more shopping... we have another commitment."

I'm reminded of the psalmist who talked about those who couldn't be bothered with seeking the Lord. He wrote: "In all his thoughts there is no room for God."[14]

So it is with many in today's world. Even on the day set aside to celebrate the birth of Jesus Christ, there's no time for Him at all. Nothing left in the schedule. No time for faith. No room at the inn.

CHRISTMAS MISCONCEPTIONS

Along with every other aspect of the Christmas story, we have romanticized this whole business of Jesus being born in a stable. These idealized (and inaccurate) perceptions have been reinforced by countless songs, movies, and depictions on Christmas cards.

As a result, we have a certain mental image when we think of that night. Generally, the whole scene is bathed in heavenly light. At the center, there's a quaint little manger with clean and dewy-eyed animals sort of bowing reverently before it. Of course, the Wise Men are there too—three of them, though Scripture never tells us how many there really were. These Magi from the East are usually dressed in color-coordinated robes, bowing and holding their gifts before them.

There's almost always an angel with a halo hovering over the stable. But then everyone else has halos too. Even the cows and sheep. It's such an idyllic scene, with Mary on one side, Joseph on the other, and a smiling, golden-haired baby Jesus in the middle.

What a lovely picture.

So calm. . . so bright. . . so pretty. . . and so wrong.

I'm not in any way making light of this holy scene; I'm simply seeking to point out how different reality would have been from this "prettied-up" notion of a stable. Say what you will, a barn was no place for a woman to have a baby. It would be like telling someone who was pregnant and having contractions, "You can sleep in the garage tonight. . . in the cold. . . on the cement. . . with the dogs."

I remember when we experienced the birth of our first grandchild, Stella. There were probably twenty family members and friends waiting outside the birthing room. And all of us were just waiting to hear the cry of the baby.

Finally, a nurse said, "You can come in now." And we all went in, so excited and happy. It was a spotlessly clean, sanitary environment, with a doctor and nurses and all of the medical equipment you can imagine in case something went wrong. And there was a loving family waiting to welcome this little baby into the world.

Compare that to the Bethlehem stable. Most likely it was cold, damp, and unsanitary. Quite frankly, the smell of animal urine probably filled the air. And that is where the Savior of the world was born. Does that spoil the picture for you? It doesn't for me. These realities in no way diminish the story. In fact, they enhance it.

The Wise Men were certainly not present at the stable that night. They came later. Matthew's Gospel tells us about them, making it clear that they came to a house, not a manger, and to a child, not a baby. Presumably the Wise Men arrived up to two years after this Bethlehem scene.

No room in the inn. When you think about it, that pronouncement before our Lord's birth symbolizes His whole life on this earth, from the cradle to the cross to a borrowed tomb.

A RUDE AWAKENING

Jesus Christ could have been born in the most elegant mansion on the ritziest boulevard in the Roman Empire. He could have had aristocratic parents boasting of their pedigree or college degrees. He could have had the finest clothes from the most exclusive shops. He could have had armies of angels to respond to His beck and call. But He didn't; He laid it all aside for us.

Think about it. When the baby eyes of Jesus fluttered open for the first time, they saw the dim and dingy outlines of a stable. The first sensation on the Baby's tender skin was the rough, torn cloth He was wrapped in. The first sound those little ears heard was probably an ox or donkey munching hay. The first smell He would have become aware of was the rank stench of a barnyard.

What a rude awakening. The fact that there was no room for Him in the inn was indicative of the treatment He would receive through all the days of His life on earth.

There is one telling passage in the Gospel of John that speaks of a night when "everyone went to his own house." But then in direct contrast it goes on to say, "But Jesus went to the Mount of Olives."[15] In other words, when everybody else called it a night and headed for hearth and fire and the comforts of home, Jesus slept out in the open air on the Mount of Olives. Our Lord said, "Foxes have holes and birds of the air have nests, but the Son of Man has nowhere to lay His head."[16]

During the three years of His ministry, Jesus would be turned away on every hand. Isaiah prophesied that He would be "despised and rejected by men, a man of sorrows, and familiar with suffering."[17] Yet it was a sacrifice He willingly made for you and me, the ultimate gift to humanity. His pain was our gain.

Even though the circumstances of our Lord's birth were poor and humble, we must not lose sight of the fact that this was a day of great, heaven-shaking joy. That is the message the angels delivered to the shepherds keeping watch over their flocks by night: "I bring you good tidings of great joy which will be to all people."

A Word about Those Shepherds

The shepherds in the Christmas story have also been overly romanticized through the years. We love that picture of shepherds watching over their sheep; it takes us back to every children's Christmas program we have ever seen. But to truly grasp the significance of the angels' announcement that night, we need to understand the actual place of shepherds in that culture.

Think about it. The angels went to some shepherds first. How amazing. Heaven's first order of business was to alert some guys way out in the pastures hanging out with a bunch of dirty sheep. The angels didn't go to Caesar's court with this message. They didn't pay a call to Herod's grand palace or visit with the religious leaders or key influential people of that day. They went to people who were the lowest of the low on the social ladder.

The truth is, shepherds were despised in that culture. So much so that the testimony of a shepherd wasn't even allowed in a court of law. The only people lower than the shepherds at this particular time in Jewish history were lepers. Yet these are the ones to whom the angels came.

I love that. If man had written the script, it would have been a different story, with bright lights, celebrities, star power, and lots of press coverage. But God had a different plan. And when those radiant messengers of heaven came to declare the best news anyone had ever heard, they came to a group of down-and-outers, in the middle of the night, on the back side of a Judean desert.

To me, this symbolizes the ministry of Jesus. He was always reaching out to the rejects and retreads of society. The Zacchaeuses of the world who had no friends. The woman at the well. The woman caught in the act of adultery. The prostitute who washed His feet with her tears. The lepers and the blind and the disabled. Unknown people. Common people. These were the people He found time for and reached out to. He cared deeply for people the "in group" wouldn't even acknowledge on the street. It's only appropriate, then, that the announcement of His birth was initially made to shepherds keeping watch over their flocks by night. They became the first heralds of the birth of Jesus.

Here is the message that was delivered to them.

Now there were in the same country shepherds living out in the fields, keeping watch over their flock by night. And behold, an angel of the Lord stood before them, and the glory of the Lord shone around them, and they were greatly afraid. Then the angel said to them, "Do not be afraid, for behold, I bring you good tidings of great joy which will be to all people. For there is born to you this day in the city of David a Savior, who is Christ the Lord. And this will be the sign to you: You will find a Babe wrapped in swaddling cloths, lying in a manger."

*And suddenly there was with the angel a multitude
of the heavenly host praising God and saying:*

*"Glory to God in the highest, and on earth peace,
goodwill toward men!"*

*So it was, when the angels had gone away from them
into heaven, that the shepherds said to one another,
"Let us now go to Bethlehem and see this thing that has
come to pass, which the Lord has made known to us."*
(Luke 2:8-15)

WHERE IS THE JOY?

Maybe you're going through some deep waters right now,
and it's a difficult time for you. It's hard for you to identify
with "good tidings of great joy."

I was speaking with a police officer the other day, and he
told me about a recent suicide. Just days before Christmas, a
despondent man took his own life. The officer reminded me
that suicides definitely spike around this time of the year.

Christmas can be a sad and unhappy time for many people.
You look at people celebrating all around you, and you feel left
out. Or you see people with what seem to be ideal marriages
and families, and you wonder what happened to yours.

We all need to get back to the original idea of what
Christmas is all about: joy. Why? Because a Savior has
been born. In Luke 1:28, when Gabriel appeared to Mary
to announce that she was to be the mother of the Messiah,
he said to her, "Rejoice, highly favored one." And that is
exactly did what Mary did in Luke 1:46, saying, "My
spirit has rejoiced in God my Savior."

THE CONDITION OF JOY

The shepherds heard the angels say to them, "We bring you good tidings of great joy."[18] Not just joy, but great joy. This famous second chapter of Luke's Gospel offers us three specific ways to discover (or rediscover) joy in Christmas.

If you want to have joy this Christmas, don't be afraid. Why? Because fear and anxiety can rob us of our joy. We think of the times we live in today as fearful times, particularly since the United States has become the target of terrorist attacks. But it wasn't exactly a Sunday school picnic in first-century Israel, either.

Those shepherds had a lot to be afraid of.

They were living under the reign of the tyrant Herod, who could execute people at will. As Jews living in a land occupied by a foreign power, there was always uncertainty about the future. Most likely, they wondered if Rome would ever leave. Would they ever be free again? And more importantly, would the Messiah ever come?

Of course, having an angel announce the arrival of the Messiah was frightening in and of itself. One of the most common angelic opening statements to earth-dwellers was, "Fear not." That's because the most common human reaction to seeing an angel was to freak out! So the angel had to reassure the shepherds a bit before delivering that great and joyful news.

I've mentioned our national worries about terrorism. But maybe you've been wrestling with some personal fears as well. What if I lose my job? What if the economy goes south? What if my health gives out? What if my marriage crumbles?

What if I can't pay off these credit cards that I have overcharged for the Christmas presents I have bought?

You could write on countless American gravestones the epitaph, "Hurried, Worried, and Buried."

Are you anxious or filled with fear right now? The message of Christmas is don't be afraid, but instead let great joy fill your heart.

The great Bible teacher Ray Stedman wrote these words:

> *The chief mark of the Christian ought to be the absence of fear and the presence of joy. We have often quoted the description of a Christian as one who is completely fearless, continually cheerful and constantly in trouble. It is that presence of joy and absence of fear that marks our genuine Christianity and proves that we really are what we claim to be.*[19]

The condition of heaven-sent joy is to let go of your fear. You can't hold them both at the same time.

The Call of Joy

In essence, the angel was telling the shepherds, "Go ahead and rejoice whether you feel like it or not, because your world has just changed forever!"

There are many reasons to be joyful this Christmas season. For starters, it's good for you! It's beneficial for your health. Proverbs 17:22 tells us, "A cheerful heart is good medicine, but a broken spirit saps a person's strength."[20]

Did you know that having the joy of the Lord is one of the most powerful magnets in your life for the gospel?

It was Friedrich Nietzsche, the atheist and German philosopher, who once said to some Christians, "If you want me to believe in your redeemer, you are going to have to look a lot more redeemed."

Do you look redeemed? Can people look at you and tell that you are a true believer? It is a powerful testimony when Christians reflect a calm and joyful spirit even in the midst of adversity.

Remember the account of Paul and Silas, who were thrown into a dungeon in Philippi for preaching the gospel? First, they were savagely beaten. Then they were put into chains and stocks. Humanly speaking, there wasn't much hope of their ever getting out.

But when we talk about the truths of the Bible, it's a lot more than "humanly speaking." With God, there is always hope. The book of Acts tells us, "At midnight Paul and Silas were praying and singing hymns to God, and the prisoners were listening to them."[21]

That's an interesting phrase... "the prisoners were listening." It could better be translated, "They were listening with pleasure." What happens when you hear your favorite song or praise chorus in church or on the radio? You say, "I love this song." Maybe you stop what you're doing to just listen. And you look forward to hearing it again.

These prisoners were listening with pleasure because they had never heard anything quite like this. Paul and Silas were singing praises to God.

Then an earthquake came, one so violent that it shook the very foundations of the prison. Chains fell off of the prisoners' hands and legs, and the doors flew open.

The Roman jailer knew that if those prisoners got away, he would forfeit his own life. In despair, he thought he might as well get it over with and commit suicide on the spot. But no one had escaped! Paul and Silas called out to the jailer, and said, "Do yourself no harm, for we are still here."

Trembling with emotion, the jailer said, "Sirs, what must I do to be saved?" In other words, "I've been watching you guys, and I want what you have. I need it right now." He was interested in Christianity because they were able to rejoice even when times were hard.

This is a wonderful magnet the Lord has given to us. The nonbeliever has nothing like it. Sure, they have their occasions of happiness, but those moments come and go. Their happiness is completely dependent on their circumstances. The joy that we experience in Christ can be ours whether we are in good times or bad.

That doesn't mean you need to walk around with a forced smile pasted on your face all day long. I've had people see me in markets and come up to me and say, "Pastor Greg, why aren't you smiling?"

"Sorry," I will say. "It was just such a deep decision. Should I get Rice Krispies or Cheerios? I forgot to smile."

Of course, it doesn't mean we have to have a plastic grin on our face 24/7! When the Bible speaks of joy, it speaks of something far deeper than that. It is an abiding joy that's there no matter what. You might say, "How can I have joy? I'm having a hard time this Christmas. I have so many problems right now... problems in my career, problems in my marriage, problems with my health. I can't be joyful."

Yes, you can. And here is why. . . .

THE CAUSE OF JOY

Look at verse 11. "There is born to you this day in the city of David a Savior, who is Christ the Lord." Underline three words: Savior. Christ. Lord. What is this saying? If you want to have joy, have it for this reason—You have a Savior. Jesus came to save you from the power and penalty of sin. Whatever you are going through in life, remember that you have a Savior. He has taken your sin and He has put it as far away from you as the east is from the west.

You have a Christ. The name Christ means "anointed one" or Messiah. Jesus is the fulfillment of God's promises to the Jewish people to send His Son as the Messiah. It is a reminder that God keeps His promises. You have a Savior who has forgiven you of your sin, and you have a Messiah who keeps His promises.

You have a Lord. Not just a companion. Not just a buddy. You have a Lord, which means you have a Leader to tell you which way to go in life. Someone to say, "Watch out for this. Here is what you need to concentrate on." Someone who will direct you in the way you should go and protect you as you head down that road. Someone who will welcome you into heaven when you have finished this course.

And one final thing in verse 11: "There is born to you this day in the city of David a Savior." This day. We might think, "I'll be happy tomorrow. I'll breathe easier next week when my next paycheck comes in, because I'm overextended. I'll be happy and joyful when I see what I get for Christmas. Hopefully my parents picked up on all of those hints I left. I can't be joyful until then." Or,

"When I finally get through this present trial, then I'll be able to smile again."

Not necessarily! After you come out of the trial you are in now, there will be another one around the corner, perhaps sooner rather than later. That's not pessimism, that's reality on planet earth.

Coming back to Ray Steadman's statement, "A Christian is one who is completely fearless, continually cheerful and constantly in trouble," it's always going to be something. Don't you know that by now? If you're not going through some kind of difficulty, either you are not breathing or you are in major denial. We all have problems in life. Don't feel like you're the exception. But rejoice anyway.

You say, "I'll rejoice when I get through this trial." No. Rejoice when you are in the trial. In fact, you are commanded to do so. In Philippians 4:4, the apostle Paul says, "Rejoice in the Lord always. Again I will say, rejoice." In the original language, it's neither a suggestion nor a pleasant devotional thought—it's a command.

By the way, when Paul penned those words, he wasn't lying on some beach sipping an iced tea with a tiny umbrella in the glass. He wasn't sitting in some ivory tower spinning off theories. These words were written by a man who knew hardship as few of us will ever know it. He was a man who had a lot to potentially worry about.

When he actually wrote those words to the Philippians, his circumstances were nothing to rejoice about. He had wanted to go to Rome to preach, but instead he was there as a prisoner. Now he waited for his case to come up and his fate to be determined. There was a chance he might be acquitted. Then again, there was an equal chance he might be beheaded. Or boiled in oil. Or tossed to the lions in the Colosseum. In Rome, you never really knew for sure.

Besides that, there were some Christian brothers who had turned against him. Close friends had become enemies, beginning a whispering campaign against the apostle while he was in prison and couldn't defend himself. But even in the midst of such bleak circumstances, Paul says to the Philippians (and all of us), "I have a message for you: Lighten up! Rejoice in the Lord always." In other words, he's saying, "If anyone has reason to be depressed, it is me. But I am not depressed. And you don't have to be either." You have a Savior. You have a Messiah. You have a Lord. That is all you need to have a joyful Christmas right now.

C. S. Lewis made this statement years ago: "God designed the human machine to run on Himself. He Himself is the fuel our spirits were designed to burn, the food our spirits were designed to feed on. There is no other. That is why it is no good asking God to make us happy in our own way without bothering about faith. God cannot give us a happiness and peace apart from Himself because it is not there. There is no such thing."

If you are looking to this world to make you happy, you never will be. If you are looking to your husband or wife or friends to make you happy, you never will be. If you are looking to Christmas to make you happy, you never will be.

You need to know Christ. That is the answer.

Christmas isn't about gifts under the tree. It's about the gift on the tree. The Bible says, "Cursed is every man that hangs on a tree." Jesus hung there in shame and disgrace, taking upon Himself all of the curse and penalty of our sins. That is the gift that God offers you: The gift of eternal life and the promise of lasting joy.

Happiness is obviously something of great importance to us as Americans. We have written it into our Declaration of Independence. It is our right to seek after life, liberty, and the pursuit of happiness.

USA Today recently did an article on happiness, interviewing hundreds of people and so-called experts to determine what the traits of a happy person are. They actually came up with some interesting conclusions.

1. HAPPY PEOPLE ALWAYS HAVE FAMILY AND FRIENDS AROUND THEM.

Long-term research proves that marriage makes people happier, and a close family inoculates many kids against despair. The happiest people always have good friends.

2. MATERIAL THINGS WILL NOT MAKE YOU HAPPY.

One expert said, "Materialism is toxic for happiness." This is especially difficult during the holidays because we can set our desire on getting certain things, and if we don't get those particular items we feel that we're not going to have a good Christmas. We have set ourselves up for disappointment. The authors of the study found that happy people did not necessarily need "things" to make them so.

3. HAPPY PEOPLE ARE ALWAYS GRATEFUL PEOPLE.

"Gratitude has a lot to do with life satisfaction," psychologists say. Talking and writing about what you are grateful for actually amplifies happiness. Other researchers have found that learning to savor small pleasures has the same effect.

4. FORGIVING PEOPLE ARE HAPPY PEOPLE.

"Forgiveness is strongly linked to happiness," says University of Michigan psychologist Christopher Peterson. He says, "It is the queen of all virtues and probably the hardest to come by."

5. THE HAPPIEST PEOPLE ON EARTH ARE SCANDINAVIANS.

So let's put it all together. You need to be forgiving. You need to be grateful. You need to have family and friends. And you need to be Scandinavian. (There's not much most of us can do about that last one.)

It's interesting how the "discoveries" in this article parallel principles we find in the Bible. To anyone who knows God's Word, this all sounds familiar. Family. Thankfulness. Forgiveness. These are certainly biblical truths.

Christmas, so it is supposed, is the happiest time of the year. I don't know who wrote that song, "It's the Most Wonderful Time of the Year," but I am convinced they have never been to a mall during Christmas.

Happiness and joy are certainly ours to experience, at Christmas and always. But it's not a mere holiday or a particular numbered square on a calendar that will lift our hearts. The joy comes to us as a living Person.

"What Must I Do?"

In Matthew 19, we read about a young man who wanted very much to find more fulfillment and joy in life. And give him credit, the first thing he did was the right thing. He came to Jesus. Here's how the Bible describes that encounter.

Someone came to Jesus with this question: "Teacher, what good deed must I do to have eternal life?"

"Why ask me about what is good?" Jesus replied. "There is only One who is good. But to answer your question—if you want to receive eternal life, keep the commandments."

"Which ones?" the man asked.

And Jesus replied: "'You must not murder. You must not commit adultery. You must not steal. You must not testify falsely. Honor your father and mother. Love your neighbor as yourself.'"

"I've obeyed all these commandments," the young man replied. "What else must I do?"

Jesus told him, "If you want to be perfect, go and sell all your possessions and give the money to the poor, and you will have treasure in heaven. Then come, follow me."

But when the young man heard this, he went away very sad, for he had many possessions. (vv. 16-22)

This young man had pretty much everything that this world has to offer, but there was something missing in his life. He had not found fulfillment in things. By all the common measurements, he should have been happy and fulfilled. But he wasn't. There was a gaping empty place in his heart.

Luke's Gospel identifies him as a ruler. The word translated "ruler" could also be rendered as "magistrate" or "prince." To have such a position, he would have had to be at least thirty, but not much over that. He had climbed the corporate ladder of his day and reached the pinnacle of his particular profession. He was a good man, moral and religious. He was also an empty man, and he didn't know why. He came to Jesus wanting to know how to obtain eternal life, but in the back of his mind, he must have wanted a few answers for this life, too.

In answer, the Lord told him to keep the commandments.

Some people will say, "I don't know that I need Jesus Christ. I live by the Ten Commandments." Of course, my response is, "You are breaking one of them right now. You are lying through your teeth! There is not a human being on earth, myself included, who keeps the Ten Commandments. When you get down to it, no one can keep them. The Bible tells us that those commandments were given that every mouth would be stopped. In other words, the commandments were given to open our eyes and to shut our mouths.

As we look at God's righteous standards, we realize we have fallen short. Some people say, "I am moral and live a relatively good life." Really? According to whose standards?

God doesn't grade on a curve. He has set a standard for all humanity to reach. And that standard is absolute and complete perfection.

You say, "Greg, that's impossible. Nobody is perfect." You got that right. And that's where Jesus comes in.

You might ask, "Then why did Jesus tell this man to keep the commandments?"

The proper response would have been, "Lord, everybody knows the commandments are very hard to keep. I have tried and failed." But this guy is so brimming with self-confidence that he says, "I have kept all of those from my youth up." There is no way he had kept these commandments—even if he thought he had. Every one of us has broken them.

Jesus mentioned adultery to this young man. I was reading an article about a young man who went to give his confession to his priest when he was eight years old because he was convinced he had committed the sin of adultery. He said, "Father, forgive me, for I have committed adultery."

The priest thought, There's no way an eight-year-old boy has committed adultery. It turned out that the little boy thought that committing adultery meant trying to act like an adult! The priest told him, "You're okay, son. Don't worry about it."

I heard about a young boy who heard his Sunday school teacher talk about adultery in class. He went home to his dad and said, "The teacher was talking to us today and told us we should not commit agriculture. What does that mean?"

The father wisely understood what the teacher was referring to and instead of correcting the boy simply said, "Son, that means you are not supposed to plow the other man's field." That was a good answer.

Committing adultery isn't just going out and being unfaithful to your spouse. According to Jesus in the Sermon on the Mount, if you have even looked on a woman with lust in your heart, you have committed adultery. Every one of us has probably done that at some time or another.

Jesus says, "You shall not kill." Most of us would say, "I have never murdered anyone." Jesus, again in the Sermon on the Mount, said that if you have had hatred toward your brother, it is the same thing.

The point is that we have broken these commandments. This guy missed what our Lord was saying. He should have said, "Lord, I confess that I have broken those commandments again and again. I want to keep them, but I can't keep them. Help me. What should I do?"

Jesus replied, "I'll tell you what you need to do. Sell all that you have, give it away, and come follow me." That's the only time that Jesus ever said that to any person. Why did He say it in this particular case? Because this young man was possessed by his possessions. The most important thing to him was his stuff—and that was keeping him from faith in Christ and eternal life.

It won't, of course, be the same for everyone. To another person Jesus might say, "You need to break off that relationship with that guy or girl who keeps dragging you down spiritually and come and follow Me." To another He might say,

"You've made your career a god in your life, and you need to abandon it, refocus yourself, and come and follow Me." To another He might say something entirely different. It depends on whom He is speaking to. God knows your heart—better than you know it—and He sees very clearly what issues or idols are keeping you from Him.

If there is anything or anyone more important to you right now than Jesus Christ, that could be a false god that is keeping you from true faith. That was the problem with this young man. I think if he had said, "No problem, Lord, it is a done deal," Jesus would have said, "Keep the stuff. I don't care about it. I just wanted to see if you would follow Me." But this man's stuff was keeping him away.

He walked away from Jesus.

He walked away from eternal life.

He walked away from joy.

Why? Because he couldn't bring himself to let go of earthly treasures in order to gain heavenly ones. Deep down, I think he knew he was making a wrong decision. The Bible says that he went away sorrowful.

Scripture tells the story of another man in a similar situation. He too was rich and powerful. He had come to Jerusalem searching for God, but had not found Him. He obtained a scroll of the prophet Isaiah and was reading it out loud when the Lord directed a preacher named Philip to articulate the gospel to him. This man from Ethiopia, who was a cabinet member serving under the queen, understood the gospel, believed it, and was baptized that day. The Bible says that he went on his way rejoicing.

An interesting contrast. Here were two very similar men. Both affluent. Both powerful. Both famous. Both given the gospel. But one went away sad, the other went away glad. It all comes down to a step of faith.

Whatever you think this world is going to give you, you need to know it will never, never be enough. You were created and wired to know God.

I think happiness is overrated. Happiness is largely dependent upon things happening. Joy comes from Jesus Christ, regardless of your circumstances. When the angels came to those shepherds keeping watch over their flocks by night, they didn't say, "Happy Holidays, and from this night forward go shop until you drop." They said, "Do not be afraid, for behold, I bring you good tidings of great joy which will be to all people. For there is born to you this day in the City of David a Savior, who is Christ the Lord."

What was the message of the angels? Joy.

And it's yours for the asking.

THREE

A Surrendered Life

I heard a story about a little girl coming home from Sunday school one Sunday morning, very excited about the drawing she had done. Eagerly, she showed it to her mom.

"Mommy, look at the drawing that I did in Sunday school of the nativity scene. My teacher said it was the most unusual she had ever seen."

As the mom looked at this drawing, she was immediately puzzled. It was obviously a picture of an airplane in flight. "Sweetheart," she said, "this is very good. But could you explain it to me? What is this airplane?"

A little indignant, her daughter replied, "That's the flight into Egypt."

"I see," her mom replied. "So who is this mean-looking man in the cockpit flying the plane?" The little girl was exasperated. "Mom, that is Pontius the pilot."

As she studied the drawing further, the girl's mom saw a little fat man seated behind Mary on the plane. She could not figure out who this could possibly be. Finally, she asked, "Honey, who is this fat man sitting behind Mary?"

The little girl said, "Mom, that is Round Jon Virgin."

You remember, of course, that line from "Silent Night"? Round yon virgin mother and child.

Truthfully, many people have difficulty with that part of the Christmas story. They stumble over the Bible's insistence that the Son of God could be supernaturally conceived as a human being in the womb of the teenage virgin Mary. How could such a thing be possible? Some mainline denominations have sidestepped that issue by simply denying that it ever happened.

THE ALL-IMPORTANT QUESTION

Popular talk show host Larry King was once asked whom he would choose if he could interview anyone across human history. Without hesitation, King replied, "I would want to interview Jesus Christ. I would want to ask Him one question, which would be, 'Are you indeed virgin born?' The answer to that question would explain history."

Larry King is right. And if you believe the Bible, there is only one possible answer to that question. Of course He was born of a virgin. No other conclusion is possible. And that is the birth we celebrate this time of the year.

When we think of Christmas, we often just think of it as the birth of Jesus, and of course it was. But we need to understand that it was as much a departure as it was an arrival.

The Bible is clear in pointing out that Jesus Christ was and is God Himself. Jesus did not come into existence in Bethlehem. We say that Jesus was born, and in the human sense, He was. He came and took upon Himself a human body.

But unlike us, there has never been a point in time when Jesus did not exist. As He says of Himself in Revelation 22:13, "I am the Alpha and the Omega, the Beginning and the End, the First and the Last." God has no beginning and no end. Jesus has always been. Not only that, but Jesus is the One who created all things. He created everything there is. Nothing exists that he didn't make.[23] He could say to you and me as He said to Job, "Where were you when I laid the foundations of the earth? Tell me, if you know so much. . . . What supports its foundations, and who laid its cornerstone as the morning stars sang together and all the angels shouted for joy?"[24]

Jesus the Son of God has a life that extends into eternity past, and when He became a man, supernaturally conceived, that was the miracle of incarnation. It is all summed up beautifully in Philippians 2:5-8, where it says, "Let this mind be in you which was also in Christ Jesus, who, being in the form of God, did not consider it robbery to be equal with God, but made Himself of no reputation, taking the form of a bondservant, and coming in the likeness of men. And being found in appearance as a man, He humbled Himself and became obedient to the point of death, even the death of the cross."

He was equal with God, yet He laid aside the privileges of deity and walked among us as a man. When I say that He laid aside the privileges, I am not suggesting for even a moment that Jesus ceased to be God. Nevertheless, He did not utilize the considerable privileges that were His as Creator when He walked this earth. In other words, when Jesus was hungry, He would eat food like any other human being. If I was God, I would design food I could eat endlessly and never put on weight! (You can see what a self-indulgent creator I would be!)

Jesus experienced human weariness. He experienced the limitations of the human body voluntarily. He walked in our shoes. As one commentator put it, "The Eternal One caught in a moment of time. The Omnipresent corralled in a cave manger. The Omnipotent cradled as a helpless infant who would not raise His head above the straw. The Omniscience confined in a baby who would not say a word. The Christ who created the heavens and the earth cradled in a manger in a cave stable."

Some people say, "I don't know if I can really believe that." It's my belief that you have to believe it if you want to call yourself a Christian. According to a survey done by George Barna, 85 percent of the Christians surveyed believe that Jesus Christ was born to a virgin. Seventy-five percent of the people he polled who were not Christians also believed in Jesus' virgin birth. As I said, if you don't believe this foundational biblical truth, you cannot be a Christian.

You say, "I don't know if that's really true. I'm not sure this is one of the essentials for salvation." Actually, it is one of the most essential Christian beliefs. To question the virgin birth is to question the Word of God that clearly teaches it. To question the virgin birth is to question the deity of Christ. If Jesus was not supernaturally conceived in the womb of Mary, then He was not God. If He was not God, then His death on the cross really meant nothing at all.

Those who suggest that the virgin birth is impossible are essentially denying what Scripture plainly teaches—that God can and will do miracles when and where He chooses.

LESSONS FROM THE LIFE OF MARY

When the mighty angel Gabriel appeared to Zacharias the priest and told him the good news about the birth of John the Baptist, the old priest was filled with doubt. After all, he was well on in years, past the age of fathering children—as was his wife, Elizabeth. Because of this unbelief, he was struck with an inability to speak until his son was born.

Meanwhile in Nazareth, a seedy little town known for its corruption and sin, God sent the same messenger to a godly young woman named Mary. She was about to discover that she would be the virgin prophesied of in Scripture.

Talk about mission impossible! What could be more difficult than this? As Mary was about to discover, with God all things are possible. Without question, there is no other person who has ever lived on this earth who had as unique a relationship with Jesus as His mother Mary. She literally had Him in her womb and later embraced Him as Savior in her heart. She was a woman who was greatly blessed by God, and she stands as a role model for all Christian women to learn from.

Unfortunately, it seems as though people either honor and in some cases even deify Mary or they ignore her altogether. We need to find the right balance for how to view this special and godly woman.

In the New Testament, Mary is never presented as the principal figure. Jesus is. All of the New Testament references to her are directly connected to Him. Yet the fact that she is constantly associated with Him does give her a place of prominence and importance. And the Lord came to this young lady (perhaps not much older than fourteen) by sending an angel.

NOWHERE LAND

Mary was a nobody in a nothing town in the middle of nowhere. Had she lived her life as many other teens of her time, she would have married a poor man and then given birth to numerous poor children. She would never have traveled more than a few miles from her home, and she would have died like thousands of others before her. Her home, Nazareth, was a non-place.

In other words, it was one of those places that one would not so much go to as pass through. Essentially, it was a place on the way to another place. You've been in little wide spots in the road like that; it's a place where you fuel up, use the facilities, get a bite to eat, and keep moving.

Nazareth was also a wicked place—a place of pagan temples where Roman soldiers would go about their ungodly living. Nazareth was not a Norman Rockwell-type small town. Thomas Kinkade probably wouldn't be drawn to paint any of its homes. It wasn't a pretty place to live or raise a family.

To this wretched little place, God sends His angel. The great God of the whole universe chose an unknown girl living in a relatively unknown city to bring about the most known event in human history—an event that we literally divide human time by.

Of Nazareth, Martin Luther made this statement: "God might have gone to Jerusalem and picked out Caiaphas' daughter, who was fair, rich, and clad in gold-embroidered clothing, and attended by an entourage of maids waiting. But God preferred a lowly maid from a mean town."

Maybe you live in a mean town right now—a place that is hostile to the gospel. Maybe you are part of a dysfunctional family. I came from a dysfunctional family—and when you come right down to it, we are all dysfunctional apart from Christ. Maybe your family has shown hostility toward the gospel, and you are the only outspoken Christian among them. Or maybe you see that same hostility and resistance in your workplace. It could be that you feel overlooked, obscure, or uncared for. Sometimes you find yourself wondering if it's even possible to live a godly life anymore. It seems like everyone around you is compromising—even so-called committed Christians.

Mary lived a pure and godly life in an ungodly place, and you can too. The same God who gave her the power to live this life will give you that power as well.

THE BEAUTY OF HUMILITY

Another thing I love about Mary is that she was honestly surprised that God had selected her and not someone else. Look at verse 29 of Luke 1. "When she saw him, she was troubled at his saying, and considered what manner of greeting this was."

The literal sense here is that Mary kept pondering the meaning of this greeting. She was thinking to herself, *Why would he say this to me? I have done nothing to merit this kind of a blessing.*

All Israel knew that the Messiah would come. I am sure the hope and prayer of every young Jewish girl was that she would be the one to fulfill the prophecy of Isaiah 7:14, "the Lord Himself will give you a sign: Behold, the virgin shall conceive and bear a Son, and shall call His name Immanuel." To think that you would even be alive when the woman was chosen would be glorious. To think that you might actually know the person who would be the mother of the Messiah would be over-whelming. But to think that you would be that person!

Imagine, girls, if God selected you for this privilege. What would your reaction be to hearing that you would bear the Messiah, the Savior of the world, God incarnate, in your womb? What an amazing thought to consider.

I love Mary's humility. She didn't say, "Well, it's about time that someone noticed my godly lifestyle. I always knew I would be the mother of the Messiah. No one else around here is living an uncompromised life but me." Of course not. She was absolutely stunned.

This reminds us that when God chooses a man or a woman, that individual should always be genuinely surprised that the Lord would select him or her. God looks for humble people, people who see themselves as they really are. A truly spiritual person will never boast of their great devotion or holiness.

When God called the prophet Isaiah, he cried out, "My doom is sealed, for I am a foul-mouthed sinner, a member of a sinful, foul-mouthed race; and I have looked upon the King."[25]

When God put His finger on Jeremiah, the young prophet felt overwhelmed: "Ah, Sovereign LORD... I do not know how to speak; I am only a child."[26]

I am always suspicious of people who brag about how committed they are. They will drop little hints like, "When I was in prayer today for three hours—my knees are still sore—but anyway, when I was in prayer interceding, the Lord reminded me of how sacrificial my tithe was last week. I don't want to put a number on it, but it was a lot. I was also thinking about how many people I have led to the Lord." What are you talking about? You should never boast of what you have done for God. Boast of what God has done for you!

I think if you are a spiritual man or woman, you will be aware of this simple fact: You have a long ways to go and you have a lot to learn. I know I do. After years of walking with the Lord, the apostle Paul referred to himself as "the chief of sinners." In Philippians he says,

I don't mean to say that I have already achieved these things or that I have already reached perfection. But I press on to possess that perfection for which Christ Jesus first possessed me. No, dear brothers and sisters, I have not achieved it, but I focus on this one thing:

Forgetting the past and looking forward to what lies ahead, I press on to reach the end of the race and receive the heavenly prize for which God, through Christ Jesus, is calling us.[27]

In other words, Paul is saying, "I have so much to learn."

So Much to Learn, So Far to Grow

I feel that way too. I've been a Christian now for over thirty years, but in some ways, I feel like I'm just getting started.

If you find yourself walking into church with a spiritually self-satisfied feeling, as though you know enough, you are not in good shape spiritually. To people with this mentality, Jesus says in the book of Revelation, "You say, 'I am rich; I acquired wealth and do not need a thing.' But you do not realize that you are wretched, pitiful, poor, blind and naked."[28]

If you are truly growing in your walk with Jesus, you will always realize how much more there is to learn, and how much more your life needs to change to be like Him.

Humbly reflective, Mary thinks about this angelic greeting. She asks a reasonable question under her circumstances. To loosely paraphrase, "Excuse me, Gabriel, but with all due respect, how will this happen, considering the fact that I have never been intimate with a man? I am a virgin." She wasn't disbelieving, she was simply asking for enlightenment. It was more of a biological question: "God, how will this take place? I was wondering about the methodology of it all."

This was in direct contrast to Zacharias, who when he was told that he would have a son in his old age doubted it outright. In his case it wasn't even a miracle. It was unlikely and rather amazing, but not something that was physically impossible.

In Mary's case it was a complete physical impossibility. There was no earthly way this could happen. Yet Mary didn't question the validity of the angel's message, she just wondered (quite naturally) about the technicalities of it all.

In effect, Gabriel replied to her, "Mary, if I told you, you would never understand. This is something beyond your comprehension. God will do it. Just accept it."

In a similar way, you and I look around us at life in the 21st century, with all of its temptations and the images that bombard us, and wonder, "Is it really possible to live a committed life to Jesus Christ in this day and age?" The answer is yes—but not in your own strength!

GOD AT WORK WITHIN

Gabriel reminded Mary, "With God all things are possible." He would say the same thing to you. God is the one who will help you finish this spiritual race that you have begun.

Philippians 2:12-13 says, "Work out your own salvation with fear and trembling; for it is God who works in you both to will and to do for His good pleasure." A more literal translation of the early part of that verse would be, "Carry to the goal and fully complete your salvation, and it is God that is working in you." The Phillips translation renders verse 13: "For it is God who is at work within you, giving you the will and the power to achieve his purpose."

The idea is that I need to recognize that I can't do it in my own strength. I am a failure, and I will always fall short. I am not able to be or to do what God calls me to be and do in my own strength. I need to say, "Lord, help me."

Have you said that? Maybe you are struggling with some temptations in your life. Maybe you have caved in many times and can't believe God would help someone like you. Maybe you find that you just can't get victory in a certain area. You need to come to the Lord and say, "Lord, I am a failure. I have fallen short. Help me to do this."

The angel told Mary that the Holy Spirit would come upon her. You and I need to be filled with the Holy Spirit on a daily basis. Ephesians 5:18 says, "Be filled with the Holy Spirit." A more literal translation of that phrase would be, "I command you to be filled with the Spirit." The original Greek also speaks of something that is continuous. Essentially God is saying, "I command you to be filled with the Spirit each and every day." Just as surely as you have to put gas in your car, you have to be filled with the Spirit again and again. How else, men, can you love your wife as Christ loved the church? How else, women, can you submit to your husband as unto the Lord? How else can we be the parents we need to be? How else can we resist temptation? How can we live this Christian life apart from the power of the Holy Spirit?

With God all things are possible. That is what the Lord said to Mary. And that is what He says to us as well.

TRUST AND OBEY

Now look at verse 38 of Luke 1. "Mary said, 'Behold the maidservant of the Lord! Let it be to me according to your word.'" Mary was completely obedient. She didn't begin to understand, but she chose to obey anyway. This is the kind of attitude God is looking for in His servants. A childlike faith and obedience. A surrendered life.

God revealed His will to Mary about her future. Many of us wish He would do the same for us. He will, but I want you to notice something: Mary completely surrendered herself to His plan before she understood the how's, why's, when's, and wherefore's. When she said, "Let it be to me according to Your word," she really had no clue what it would all mean or how it would all work out. At that moment, she didn't know how Joseph would respond... or her family... or her community. The only important thing at that moment was submitting to the Lord's will.

In Romans 12:1-2, Paul says, "I beseech you therefore, brethren, by the mercies of God, that you present your bodies a living sacrifice, holy, acceptable to God, which is your reasonable service. And do not be conformed to this world, but be transformed by the renewing of your mind, that you may prove what is that good and acceptable and perfect will of God."

We immediately gravitate toward the latter part of that verse because that is something we all want to know, right? The good and acceptable and perfect will of God. But notice that God says, "If you want to know My will, surrender to Me first." Present yourself to God. Don't be conformed to the world. Be transformed by the renewing of your mind. Then you will know the will of God.

Some of us want to find out what God's will is before we submit to it. Sometimes I will say to one of my sons,

"Could you do something for me?"

And he will say, "What?"

He doesn't say "yes," he says "What?" He wants to find out what it is before he commits to it. Most of the time it's something pretty basic that I don't want to do—like take out the trash. But sometimes it will involve something that's fun... something I haven't told him about yet.

In a similar way, the Lord comes to us and says, "My son, My daughter, will you do something for Me?"

And we say "What, Lord? Tell me what it is and I'll decide if I will do it. Give me Your command and I'll decide if I want to obey it." That's not what He wants to hear. What He wants to hear is, "Yes, Lord. I'll do what You want me to do. I trust You to lead me in the best way." When you surrender yourself to Him, He will reveal His will to you.

"Good, Acceptable, Perfect"

Notice that Romans 12:2 speaks of the good and acceptable and perfect will of God. God's will for you is good.

That's not the way the world works, is it? The world gives the sense that whatever is forbidden must be good, and whatever is allowed must be bad. It's like the adulterous woman in the book of Proverbs who says, "Stolen melons are the sweetest; stolen apples taste the best!"[29] Oh really? I think that is nothing more than a lie of the enemy.

Desserts are described as "decadent" or "sinfully delicious." The idea is that if it's fun, it must be sinful. As if the devil has all the good stuff and God just has a bunch of bland, generic, mediocre stuff. What could be further from the truth?

The Bible says, "No good thing will He withhold from those who walk uprightly."[30]

When will we learn that the devil is a L-I-A-R? He doesn't have the good stuff; the Lord does. Oh sure, the devil has some pretty, shiny trinkets here and there, but they are like bombs in children's toys. We need to submit to God and find the truth for ourselves. The condition to an enlightened mind is a surrendered heart.

Poor Mary. Her head must have been swimming. How would she explain this to her betrothed? "Umm, Joseph, I'm pregnant. But wait—let me tell you the whole story! You know that Scripture talks about the Messiah being born to a virgin woman? Well, guess what... I am the virgin. By the way, are we still on for Saturday night?"

Seriously, how could you communicate something like this? What man would believe that story? What husband-to-be would accept an explanation as amazing as that?

This is a reminder that when we are in the will of God, He will open doors for us and also confirm His will. When Joseph found out about Mary's condition, he was of course devastated. But God wasn't going to leave it like that. Because Mary had submitted to God's will, He would take care of the details with Joseph. According to Matthew's Gospel, one night while Joseph was sleeping, Gabriel appeared to him in a dream and told him the whole story. God had clearly spoken to Mary. And He confirmed it to Joseph.

It reminds us that just as important as the will of God is the timing of God. When God is leading you, He will confirm the steps you are taking. Sometimes we will pray for something and God will say no, and we wonder why.

Listen to this. If the request is wrong, God says "No."
If the timing is wrong, God says "Slow." If you are wrong,
God says "Grow." If the request is right and the timing
is right and you are right, God says "Go." If the timing
is wrong, God says to slow down, you're going too fast.
If you are wrong, God says He won't give you what you
are asking for. It would only harm you. You need to grow
up. Then when everything is in line, God will say to go.

I am sure that Mary, being human, still had her doubts.
Haven't you ever had doubts even after God has revealed
His will to you? I can imagine her thinking, *How am I
going to convince people of this? I know Joseph believes
it. But what will others say?*

She decided to go visit her cousin Elizabeth, who was
now six months pregnant with John the Baptist. Maybe
Mary was thinking on the way to Elizabeth's house, *How
am I ever going to convince Elizabeth?* Mary would soon
have her answer, as God gave her yet another confirmation.

SWEET CONFIRMATION

*Now Mary arose in those days and went into the hill
country with haste, to a city of Judah, and entered
the house of Zacharias and greeted Elizabeth. And
it happened, when Elizabeth heard the greeting
of Mary, that the babe leaped in her womb; and
Elizabeth was filled with the Holy Spirit.*

*Then she spoke out with a loud voice and said,
"Blessed are you among women, and blessed is the
fruit of your womb! But why is this granted to me,*

that the mother of my Lord should come to me?
For indeed, as soon as the voice of your greeting
sounded in my ears, the babe leaped in my womb
for joy. Blessed is she who believed, for there will
be a fulfillment of those things which were told her
from the Lord." (Luke 1:39-45)

There is an interesting contrast between these two women. They had a lot in common. Both of them had babies that were announced by the mighty angel Gabriel. Both of them would give birth to children who would fulfill Bible prophecy. Elizabeth bore in her womb the greatest prophet that would ever be in the history of Israel. Mary bore in her womb the Messiah of Israel and the Savior of the world.

What times they must have had praying together! Yet one was in the flower of her youth and one was near the end of her days. In their time together, they were able to mutually encourage each other.

Verse 41 reveals something very interesting: John, the unborn child, responded before Elizabeth did. That is fascinating! He was already starting His prophetic ministry. He couldn't wait. He was a prophet in her womb, and this was his first prophecy. John the Baptist's ministry was beginning three months before his birth, because the Holy Spirit prompted him to do this. The word that is used here for "leaped" means just that. This was not a little kick; it was a big leap. He was overcome with joy. He leaped with delight! Don't miss this.

This fetus experienced very real human emotion at six months. I hope this can help us lay to rest the fact that the Bible opposes the so-called "pro choice" position on abortion, and that life begins at conception, not at birth.

Here the Lord is just conceived, and His presence in the womb of Mary awakens John in the womb of Elizabeth and causes him to leap for joy. He has already started getting the message out that the Messiah is coming.

Then Elizabeth shouts, "Blessed are you among women, and blessed is the fruit of your womb. How is it that the mother of my Lord should come to me?" Everything was falling beautifully into place. This was all from God.

Perhaps you, like Mary, would like to be used by God someday and in some way. Then follow her example! To the best of your ability seek to live a godly life in this ungodly world. Completely surrender yourself to the will of God before you know what it is. Having discovered it, obey it. Know that the Lord will open doors for you and confirm His will in your life.

FOUR

God with Us!

Juliet asked Romeo, "What's in a name?"
And then she answered her own question.
"What's in a name? That which we call
a rose by any other name would smell as sweet."[31]

Now that may be true if you are a flower. But if you are a person, a name makes a difference, doesn't it? If you've gone through life with a name you didn't necessarily appreciate, you know how important a name can be.

Remember Johnny Cash's old song, "A Boy Named Sue"? It told the story of a dad who named his boy "Sue" so that he would be tough after fighting everyone on the planet who made fun of him.

Maybe you got stuck with a name you didn't particularly appreciate. Or maybe you had one of those nicknames attached to you that followed you well into your adult years. I had one, and I hesitate to commit it to print in this book lest you meet me in person someday and address me this way. Nevertheless, I will make the sacrifice for a point in this book. (Anything for the ministry.) Here it is.

I went through life with the nickname of "Pogo."

You have to be my age or older to understand my reference point here. Pogo was a cartoon strip in the paper years ago: "Pogo the Possum" by Walt Kelley. And I acquired this name because someone in the family (bless 'em), thought I looked like Pogo Possum when I was a baby.

Now it's fine to be called Pogo when you're four, and it's still a little cute when you're nine. But by the time you get to be twelve, it's not so cool. When you're sixteen it's very uncool. When you're twenty, it's downright irritating. When you are thirty and still can't shake the name, you want to hurt someone. My family calls me "Pogo" to this day.

Sigh.

Maybe you got stuck with some kind of a nickname in your early years. And it's funny, because parents will think so hard about what to name a child. They will agonize over a name, poring over books of names and their meanings. And then before the kid's out of diapers he gets stuck with a ridiculous nickname.

Psychologist and name expert Cleveland Evans of Nebraska's Belleview University said, "Names tell you more about the parents than about the kids. They reveal their values and goals for their children." For instance, many parents who had children in the sixties when they were living in communes and living the hippie lifestyle gave children names that reflected their values and lifestyles. You can meet people walking around today with names like Morning, Carrot, Sunshine, Fender, Gravy, or Doobie. Those are all actual names; I'm not making these up.

And it's also interesting how each generation will have certain names that, for whatever reason, become fashionable and popular. In my parents' generation, it was names like Flora, Charlene, Doris, and Margaret. Look in the obituaries of guys passing away in their seventies and eighties and you'll see handles like Fred, Seymour, Hubert, and Willard.

At this writing (it will soon change), the most popular names today for girls are Ashley, Haley, Madison, Katelyn, Hannah, and Emily—the number one girl name. For boys, people seem to be favoring the names Christopher, Joseph, Andrew, Joshua, Matthew, Nicholas, Michael, and Jacob—the number one boy's name. It's also popular these days to give girls the names of virtues, such as Faith, Grace, Hope, Charity, Mercy, Honesty, and Serenity. And stone and gem names are also popular for girls: Amber, Jade, Diamond, and Crystal. For boys, geographic names are popping up. You're hearing about Texas, Dallas, and Dakota. (I haven't heard about any California boys being named Anaheim or Bakersfield yet.)

And then there are those parents who think themselves clever and humorous when they name their children something that plays off their last names. These are actual names of people: Paige Turner, Warren Peace, Justin Case, Carl Arm (Car alarm!), Chris B. Bacon, Ilene Dover, and Gene Poole. On and on it goes. It's unreal! Can you imagine saddling a kid with a name like one of these?

Back in biblical times, names would often be given to describe events that took place at the child's birth.

The first created man, for instance, was named Adam, or Earth, because he had been formed from the dust of the ground. And remember the story in Genesis of Jacob and Esau? Esau meant "hairy," because that's the way he came out of the womb. His brother, born immediately afterwards, came out holding Esau's heel. So he was named Jacob, or "heel-grabber."

In the book of Judges, there was a pregnant woman who got word that Israel's army had been defeated by the Philistines and the ark of the covenant had been taken. She was so shocked that she immediately gave birth, dying in the process. She named her baby boy Ichabod, which means, "the glory has departed." What a terrible thing to name an innocent child! Would you play with a kid named Glory-Has-Departed? I don't think I would.

Then again, sometimes people in Scripture didn't have any choice of what to name their son or daughter, because God told them in advance what the child would be called. And that was the case with Mary and Joseph, who experienced two separate visitations by an angel of the Lord... who left no doubt at all what their son would be named.

"YOU SHALL CALL HIS NAME..."

"Mary... will bring forth a Son, and you shall call His name Jesus, for He will save His people from their sins" (Matthew 1:21). Jesus. It's really the same as "Joshua," and it means "Jehovah is salvation." It is the name that is above every name. It is the name that divides human time, and it is the name before which all the world will one day bow and give honor.

The Bible says,

> *Therefore God also has highly exalted Him and given*
> *Him the name which is above every name, that at*
> *the name of Jesus every knee should bow, of those in*
> *heaven, and of those on earth, and of those under the*
> *earth, and that every tongue should confess that Jesus*
> *Christ is Lord, to the glory of God the Father.*
> *(Philippians 2:8-11)*

There is so much in the name of Jesus for us to discover. I think we will have all eternity to do that, and we will never come to the end of its majesty and wonder.

The prophet begins that process for us in the ninth chapter of Isaiah. These are words that were penned seven hundred years before the birth of Jesus. But in this prophetic passage often cited in the Christmas season, Isaiah gives us a glimpse into the mighty Name. In each of Isaiah's descriptions, he teaches us an attribute of God. Here is the familiar passage:

> *For unto us a Child is born,*
> *Unto us a Son is given;*
> *And the government will be upon His shoulder.*
> *And His name will be called Wonderful, Counselor,*
> *Mighty God, Everlasting Father, Prince of Peace.*
> *Of the increase of His government and peace*
> *There will be no end.*
> *(Isaiah 9:6-7)*

Look at verse 6 again. "Unto us a Child is born, unto us a Son is given." The story of Jesus Christ coming into this world is not so much the story of a birth as it is the story of a gift. For us, you see, it was the entrance of Jesus to the planet earth. But for the Father, it was the departure of His Son from heaven. The Son was given... to us! The first Christmas was not a gift to a child, it was the gift of a child. Jesus said, "For God so loved the world that He gave His only begotten Son, that whoever believes in Him should not perish but have everlasting life."[32]

Because Jesus was born into the human race in Bethlehem, we sometimes think of that event as His entrance into the universe. But we need to understand that the birth of Jesus was not His beginning. It was rather His entrance into the space and time of this world as the Messiah of Israel and the Savior of the world.

Because Jesus is Himself God, He had no beginning. Along with God the Father and the Holy Spirit, He always was—without beginning or end. In Micah 5:2, a Scripture we've already looked at, the prophet describes the coming Messiah as one "Whose goings forth are from of old, from everlasting."

But it's even more mind-boggling than that. God not only became a man, He first became an embryo in Mary's womb. And then, like every other baby, He was carried full-term and born in the natural way. And you know what? When Jesus was born, He was a baby like any other baby. He didn't have a halo, and He wasn't born with fully developed ability to speak.

The Bible never says that baby Jesus looked up from the manger and said, "Why, hello there Mary, Joseph. How are you? I am Jesus Christ, and you don't have to change My diaper, and I will walk immediately. That's because I'm God in human form, and I have to get on with My ministry."

That's not what happened. Jesus was a little baby dependent on a mother for nourishment. He grew up like any other child, though He was without sin and was truly God in human form. Who can wrap their minds around all this?

And then Isaiah continues, saying, "And you shall call His name Wonderful, Counselor, the Mighty God, the Everlasting Father, the Prince of Peace." When you stop and think about it, each of these descriptions of Jesus' name deals with an important area of our lives.

I am indebted to Warren Wiersbe, and his insightful book *His Name is Wonderful*, for my outline here.

His name is Wonderful. That takes care of the dullness of life. We no longer have to look to this world for shallow excitement or cheap substitutes for fulfillment. Jesus Christ makes life wonderful.

His name is Counselor. That takes care of the decisions of life. You no longer have to be baffled by the problems of life, wondering what step to take next. With Jesus Christ as our Counselor, we have the wisdom we need to make the decisions, both great and small, which confront us each day.

His name is Mighty God. That takes care of the demands of life. Sometimes we can be overwhelmed with all that life dishes out. But we must never forget that no matter what we face, we are linked to the Mighty One, the all-powerful Lord Jesus. And Scripture reminds us that we can do all things through Christ who strengthens us.[32]

His name is Everlasting Father. That takes care of the future. Knowing that as Christians we will spend all eternity with Him, we don't have to be afraid of death.

His name is the Prince of Peace. That takes care of the disturbances of life. Certainly we live in frightening times, but with Christ in residence in the very center of our being, we can know a peace that "is far more wonderful than the human mind can understand."[34]

Because each of these portraits of Jesus is so filled with richness and wonder, let's go back over each name a little bit more slowly.

HIS NAME IS. . . WONDERFUL

The word wonderful comes from the root word wonder.

Bertrand Russell claimed that at least half of the sins of mankind were caused by the fear of boredom. As a society, we have never been more technologically advanced. The flow of new developments, new trends, new discoveries in science and technology, and new gadgets and entertainments is like water from a fire hydrant—it's overwhelming. We have our TVs, our CDs, our DVDs, our DVDRWs, our MP3s, our iPods, iPhones, and PDAs. If we get tired of fooling with those things, we've got our Gamecubes, Nintendo 64s, Xboxes, Sony Playstations, PSPs, and all the rest of it. And amazingly, despite all of this technology, you will still hear kids say, "I'm bored!"

Have you ever walked into a room and seen a teenager sitting in front of a TV, talking on a cell phone, instant-messaging, and playing a computer game all at the same time? This is the kind of world our children are being raised in today.

You may lay down a pile of money to acquire the latest and greatest electronic gadget and be thrilled with it for a week or two. But then all too quickly the newer version comes out, rendering your device outdated, obsolete, second-class, and uncool. Before long, you set it aside because it no longer occupies your attention. It's lost its allure.

Why do man-made marvels fail to satisfy us? Because we were created to interact with an all-wise, all-powerful, infinitely beautiful, constantly engaging God. We were hardwired to know Him, experience Him, walk with Him, and enjoy Him. And He is wonderful like nothing else in the entire universe is wonderful. That means that, apart from Him, there is nothing in this world that will satisfy the deepest needs of your life.

Actress Meg Ryan was recently interviewed in *Us Magazine*. The interviewer asked her this insightful question: "You seem to have the life that most people would dream of. The work you enjoy. Your marriage. Your children. Your fame and your wealth. Yet it didn't really make you happy, did it?"

And Meg Ryan replied, "No, it didn't content me. I never think of myself as someone who got the brass ring. I think of myself as someone who is constantly in search of—of what I don't know. It feels like a constant forward motion toward what I am afraid of or the unknown. There always comes some other thing I haven't done, some other place I haven't been to, some other person I haven't met. I have never had the time where I sat back and felt satisfied like now I have got it."

If we think that one accomplishment, one honor, one experience, one possession, or one relationship will finally satisfy us and fill the void within us, we will always be disappointed. No matter what this world offers, it will always fall short. But when you know God, when you know the Savior whose name is Wonderful, He will satisfy the deepest needs of your life.

As I contemplate this wonderful God and the sacrifice He made for me, it produces a sense of awe, wonder, bewilderment, and yes, finally, worship. David said it so well in one of his psalms. Looking up into the seemingly endless depths of a starry night sky, he sang:

> *When I consider Your heavens,*
> *the work of Your fingers,*
> *The moon and the stars, which You have ordained,*
> *What is man that You are mindful of him,*
> *And the son of man that You visit him?*
> *(Psalm 8:3-4)*

Knowing this wonderful God personally takes care of the dullness of life. While medical science will attempt to add years to your life, only Jesus Christ can add life to your years. His name will be called Wonderful. Do you know Him in that way?

HIS NAME IS... COUNSELOR

Psalm 73:24 says, "You will guide me with Your counsel, and afterward receive me to glory." Did you know that God wants to give personal counsel and direction to you?

Again, in Psalm 33 He promises us, "I will instruct you and teach you in the way you should go; I will guide you with My eye."

Some will go down to the local bar and pour out their troubles to anyone who will listen. Others in desperation will call television psychics for some kind of direction in life, or spend thousands and thousands on therapy or the latest prescription drugs in their search for answers.

Yet here is the Almighty God, the Everlasting Father, Jesus Christ offering you His counsel. He wants to direct you. Here is a Counselor who has known you from the foundations of the world, watched your life since conception, and knows the future as intimately as He does the past. The Bible says, "If any of you lacks wisdom, let him ask of God, who gives to all liberally and without reproach."[35]

When is the last time you just opened up the Book and said, "Lord, speak to me"? The Bible is the user's manual of the life we've all been searching for. Within its pages you'll find answers for how to have a successful marriage... how to function in the workplace... how to strengthen your relationships... how to raise your children... how to view the times in which we live... how to handle depression, temptation, and loneliness... how to build a value system that will bless and elevate your life for the rest of your years. Everything you need to know about God is found in the pages of the Bible.

Paul wrote to Timothy, "All Scripture is inspired by God and is useful to teach us what is true and to make us realize what is wrong in our lives. It corrects us when we are wrong and teaches us to do what is right. God uses it to prepare and equip his people to do every good work."[36]

HIS NAME IS... MIGHTY GOD

Jesus Christ was not just a good man, He was (and is) the God-man. God with us! In fact, this was one of the primary reasons He was condemned and crucified, in that His accusers said, "He continually made Himself equal to God."

He did that, and it was true! He is the Mighty God, with unlimited power. Now power is a very appealing thing, especially if you're a guy. Guys love power. If you have a car, another guy sees it and says, "What have you got under the hood? How fast is it?" Or if you have a computer, "How fast is that thing? How many megahertz? How many gigs of storage?" Or if you go to the gym, "Yeah, well how much can you bench? How many curls can you do? How many sit-ups or push-ups can you do?" It's all about power.

Maybe you've seen the *Lord of Rings* movies. The first installment of the trilogy, *The Fellowship of the Ring*, tells the story of a special ring that gives tremendous power to the person who wears it. But each one who gets hold of this ring becomes corrupted by it... except for one little hobbit named Frodo. He is the only one who could wear the ring and not be turned evil by its great power.

J. R. R. Tolkien's tale is an imaginative picture of the real world. The history of mankind has been the story of discovering, using, and abusing power. First there was manpower, then horsepower, then steam power, then nuclear power. But what we seem to be lacking is willpower—the power to control ourselves.

But we have the Mighty God who wants to get involved in our lives, giving us the internal energy to do what He wants us to do and be what He wants us to be.

Honestly, have you ever found it difficult to be a Christian? At times, I certainly have. Sometimes it's hard to resist temptation. Sometimes it's hard to go the extra mile. Sometimes it's hard to forgive and return kindness for personal attacks. Sometimes it's hard to be consistent in reading the Word and spending time in prayer.

But you need to know that the Almighty God will give you the power to live the life He has called you to live. Otherwise, He wouldn't ask you to do these things. The fact is, you cannot live this Christian life in your own strength, and neither can I. No one can. But Jesus is "Mighty God," and He lives within us, helping us to follow Him and live the life He calls us to live.

The Bible says, "Work out your own salvation with fear and trembling; for it is God who works in you both to will and do for His good pleasure." Another translation of that same verse reads, "It is God who is at work within you, giving you the will and the power to achieve his purpose."[37]

Perhaps you're struggling right now with some kind of vice. Maybe you would say, "I've really tried to stop smoking." Or, "I've tried to stop drinking." Or, "I've tried to be free from the power of drugs. I've tried everything." Or, "I'm hooked on pornography, and I can't break free." You need to go to your knees and say, "Lord, I can't do it on my own. I need Your help. I need Your power in my life. I have tried, and I have failed." The One whose name is Mighty God will help you.

HIS NAME IS... EVERLASTING FATHER

The name of Jesus reminds us that we will indeed live forever with Him—that there is hope beyond the grave. The hope of a heavenly Father or an Everlasting Father resonates with some of us who perhaps never had an earthly father.

I never knew who my dad was when I was growing up. Later in life, I found out that I'd been born out of wedlock. Some people call children like me "illegitimate," but I know better. I know that from the very moment of my conception, my Everlasting Father had a plan for my life, regardless of the way that I came about. And I know that even though I never had an earthly father to provide the guidance I wanted in life, I had a heavenly Father who loved me and cared for me.

Maybe you've come from a family where your parents have split up, or your mom or dad has abandoned you in some way. You need to know there is an Everlasting Father who is there for you.

HIS NAME IS... PRINCE OF PEACE

In the storms of life, we all long for peace within. These are turbulent times in our nation's history, with war on the other side of the world, the constant threat of terrorism at home, and violent crime in our cities and neighborhoods. It's unsettling. Disturbing.

And here in the season when we celebrate the arrival of the Prince of Peace, we recall the message the angels gave so many years ago: "Glory to God in the highest, and on earth peace among men with whom He is pleased."[38]

We look around at the world and say, "Where is it? Where is the peace on earth?"

Maybe we should give more careful attention to what the angels actually said. They said, "Peace on earth among men with whom He is pleased." Isn't it obvious? The reason we don't have peace is that we don't please God! It's because of our sinful temperaments and the bent in us to do the wrong thing that we have such turmoil in our world today.

But we can know the Prince of Peace. And not only that, God promises you personal peace. In the book of Philippians, God gives us an amazing roadmap to peace within. I quoted this verse from Philippians a little earlier, but here it is in its full context:

> *Don't worry about anything; instead, pray about everything. Tell God what you need, and thank him for all he has done. Then you will experience God's peace, which exceeds anything we can understand. His peace will guard your hearts and minds as you live in Christ Jesus.*[39]

How practical can you get? The Bible just lays it out for us here. And you can't get this kind of peace from a pill or out of a bottle. Do you have peace like that right now?

THE GOVERNMENT UPON HIS SHOULDERS

As happens so often in Old Testament prophetic passages, a wide valley of human history stretches between the two mountain peaks in the first and second parts of Isaiah 9:6.

First the prophet says, "Unto us a Child is born, unto us a Son is given." That was fulfilled when Jesus was born to Mary, in that Bethlehem stable on the first Christmas night. The next part of the verse is yet future: "And the government will be upon His shoulder."

For over 2000 years, believers have been waiting and longing for the return of Jesus Christ and the fulfillment of this verse. The government is not yet upon His shoulders... but it will be! And "of the increase of His government and peace there will be no end" (verse 7).

The Bible speaks of a coming day when Christ Himself will return to earth and establish His kingdom. There will be no more waste or corruption in government. There will be no global terrorism. There will be no more wars or rumors of wars. Jesus, God's Son will reign righteously as King of kings and Lord of lords.

But listen to this. Before taking the government upon His shoulders, He would first take a cross upon His shoulders and die upon it. And that threw most of the Jewish people for a loop.

As we've noted, most believed that the Messiah would overthrow the tyranny of Rome at last, establishing His kingdom then and there by force. But it wasn't our Lord's mission to overthrow Rome at that time. In God's eternal plan of the ages, the first thing He had to do was give up His life and die on a Roman cross for the sins of the world.

That mission of salvation and redemption was indicated back at the time when the Wise Men arrived from the East, bearing gifts for the newborn King. Remember what the Magi brought to the young Jesus? Gold, frankincense, and myrrh. Don't those seem like unusual gifts to bring to a little child? I mean, why not a stuffed camel?

But you see, these far-seeing Wise Men had an insight as to who this child was. They brought gold because they understood He would be a king. They brought frankincense or incense because they realized He would be a priest, representing us to God. And finally, they brought myrrh, which was an embalming element.

Now that is an odd gift to give to someone. Myrrh! That would be like giving someone formaldehyde for their birthday. That might be appropriate if the individual is turning forty (just kidding), but under normal circumstances most people would regard this as a strange, rather morbid gift. ("Merry Christmas. I hope you like this embalming fluid I bought you. You never know when it might come in handy!")

But they gave Jesus myrrh because these men from the East seemed to understand that this child who would be king and priest was also coming to die for the sins of the world. Before Jesus would take the government on His shoulders, He would first bear a cross upon His shoulders. He would surrender His life to ransom us from our sins and from our futile, empty lives.

But here's the good news: You don't have to wait for the return of Jesus Christ to experience His rule in your life. You can experience it today, because this Mighty God wants to be your Everlasting Father. He wants to show you how wonderful He is as He counsels you and floods your life with His peace that passes all human understanding. The government of your life can be on His shoulders, setting you free to live the life God intended for you from the beginning.

What's in a name? It all depends on whom that name belongs to. If it is the name of Jesus Christ, you have the greatest name in time and eternity. Wonderful. Counselor. Mighty God. Everlasting Father. Prince of Peace. And beyond all of that, Savior and Friend.

<hr/>

We know that Jesus came to the planet called earth. More specifically, He came to the obscure little village of Bethlehem. But the story didn't really start in Bethlehem. It began long before, in another time and another place. The time was eternity, and the place was heaven.

Even before there was a planet called earth and a creation called man, before there was a man named Adam and a woman named Eve eating forbidden fruit in a garden called Eden bringing this curse of sin on humanity— before all of that, a decision was made in heaven that God would become a man and die on our behalf.

God burst into human history at the right time. God has His own timetable; He is never late. He did it when He wanted to do it. As Galatians 4:4 says, "When the fullness of the time had come, God sent forth His Son, born of a woman, born under the law, to redeem those who were under the law." In the fullness of time, Mary supernaturally conceived in her womb the very Son of God, the Ancient of Days.

I'm reminded of the story of a little ten-year-old girl who was becoming quite knowledgeable about the Bible because of her grandmother's instruction. One day she came to her grandmother with a question. "Grandma," she said, "which virgin was the mother of Jesus: the Virgin Mary or the King James Virgin?"

The fact is, if you believe in a God who created the universe with a word, you will have no trouble at all believing that He could have His Son supernaturally conceived in the womb of the virgin. When you stop and think about it, it makes complete sense.

For instance, it was possible for God the Father to send Jesus to this earth as a complete yet sinless human being without a human parent. He could have had the heavens open, a shaft of light come out, and Jesus descend to the earth, declaring, "I am Jesus, the Son of God. I am a man like you are, but I have come from heaven." If that had happened, it would have been hard for the people of that day to believe that Jesus was actually human and could truly understand their needs, sorrows, and struggles.

On the other hand, it also would have been possible for God the Father to come into the world with two human parents, both a mother and father, with His full divine nature. But if that were the case, it would have been hard for people to believe that Jesus was indeed God, since His origin would have been like theirs in every way.

The way that God came to earth was logical. And if you don't believe this miracle, why believe in any miracle? If you don't believe this Bible account, why believe in the Bible at all?

Now the most important question of all: Why did Jesus come? Did He come to teach us the ultimate life principles? Yes, to some degree He did. But His teachings were that and more. Did He come to set the perfect example of how a man should live? Yes, Jesus lived a perfect life for all to see—the only perfect human life that has ever been lived. But that's not the primary reason He came either. Did He come to do miracles and heal people? Yes, all of that and much more. But even that is not the principal reason why He came. We love to talk about how He came. We love to focus on the miracle of His birth. But why did He come to the earth in the first place?

TO BRING US PURPOSE AND LIFE

Jesus Himself said in John 10:10, "I have come that they may have life, and that they may have it more abundantly."

From the day that you were born, you have been on a quest. You have been searching for something more. Deep down inside of you there is a sense that life must have some meaning and purpose beyond mere existence. You have often wondered, Am I the only person who feels this way? Am I the only one around who is disillusioned with the things that this world offers? There has to be something more.

There is. You need to know you were essentially heart-wired by God with the sense that there is more to life. That is why mere earthly pursuits, achievements, and pleasures will never quite fill the void deep inside of you. Jesus came to give life—life in all of its fullness on earth and life beyond the grave.

You'll just have to take my word on what I'm going to say next. Let me tell you something. If there were not a heaven, if there was no hope beyond this life, if there was nothing to be experienced as a Christian beyond what I have here and now, I would still be a follower of Jesus. I realize that Paul said, "If our hope in Christ is only for this life, we are more to be pitied than anyone in the world."[40] That's what the apostle said all right. But the way I see it (and maybe it's because I already have Jesus living inside me, giving me peace and joy at this very moment), the Christian life is still the best life there is. I have a life with purpose, meaning, and direction. I have standards and values that elevate my life and keep me from living in the gutter. I have God Himself living inside of me, helping me through each step of life.

But the good news is that there is life beyond the grave. There is a heaven. As one paraphrase renders the Lord's words, "I came so they can have real and eternal life, more and better life than they ever dreamed of."[41]

To Heal the Brokenhearted

In the gospel of Luke, Jesus said,
"The Spirit of the LORD is upon Me,
Because He has anointed Me
To preach the gospel to the poor;
He has sent Me to heal the brokenhearted."
(Luke 4:18)

Maybe you have a broken heart as you read through these pages. You feel as though no one understands or cares about you. Maybe your heart has been broken by divorce, or you've been estranged from your parents or children. At this time of year, the pain of those heartaches seems to double.

Perhaps your heart is broken because you've lost someone in this last year. My mom died right after Christmas a few years ago, and that is something I will remember.

If you have a broken heart this Christmas, God sent His Son to heal it. Jesus knows what it's like to be abandoned by friends. He understands what it's like to be let down. He has felt the sting of death. He has experienced everything you and I have experienced—apart from our sin—to show us that He can understand and heal our broken hearts.

I love how the book of Hebrews describes this:

Since we, God's children, are human beings—made of flesh and blood—he became flesh and blood too by being born in human form; for only as a human being could he die and in dying break the power of the devil who had the power of death....

We all know he did not come as an angel but as a human being—yes, a Jew. And it was necessary for Jesus to be like us, his brothers, so that he could be our merciful and faithful High Priest before God, a Priest who would be both merciful to us and faithful to God in dealing with the sins of the people. For since he himself has now been through suffering and temptation, he knows what it is like when we suffer and are tempted, and he is wonderfully able to help us. (Hebrews 2:14-18, TLB)

The primary reason that Jesus came was to forgive us of our sin. Jesus said in Matthew 20:28, "The Son of Man did not come to be served, but to serve, and to give His life as a ransom for many." That babe in the manger stood in the shadow of the cross. From the earliest parts of His ministry, He spoke repeatedly of the fact that He would die. Not just that He would die, but that He would die a painful, shameful death. And more specifically, that He would lay His life down. No one would take it from Him; He would give it of His own accord.

He came to die and give His life as a ransom for many. Why? Because Greg Laurie sinned. Because you have sinned. We have all broken His commandments time and time again, and we are separated from Him. So He sent His Son. That is what Christmas is all about.

One of the most familiar passages in the whole Bible underlines this bedrock truth: "For God so loved the world that He gave His only begotten Son, that whoever believes in Him should not perish but have everlasting life. For God did not send His Son into the world to condemn the world, but that the world through Him might be saved" (John 3:16-17).

God so loved the world. Many people envision God as a cosmic killjoy, out there wanting to rain on their parade and ruin their lives. Nothing could be further from the truth. God loves you. He longs for fellowship with you. He misses you when you sin against Him. He wants to have communion with you. Jesus said, "Greater love has no one than this, than to lay down one's life for his friends."[42]

We can talk about love all day long, we can sing about it, compose poems about it, or write the word on a wall in letters three feet high. But Jesus demonstrated—proved—His love for us by giving up His life to save us.

When God offers this ultimate gift to us and we turn it away, it is an insult. It's tragic. Take the gift that God has for you! It's a million times better than any other gift you will receive under the tree this year. Jesus said to the woman at the well, "If you only knew the gift God has for you and who you are speaking to, you would ask me, and I would give you living water."[43] The gift He offered her is the same gift He offers us—the gift of God, which is eternal life through Jesus Christ our Lord. The ultimate Gift. The indescribable Gift.

With Christmas almost upon you, the pressure mounts! But finally you place your last purchases in the trunk, back out of that precious parking space at the mall, and head for home.

"Yes!" you say to yourself. "I'm done! It's over with!"

But then, halfway home, it hits you. "Oh no! I've forgotten Aunt Harriet!" And you have to turn around, go back to the mall you just departed from in triumph, find a new parking space, and head back inside for another round.

Or maybe you receive a gift in the mail—something relatively nice—and you feel obligated to send something back. Sometimes these feelings of obligation can take all the fun out of it for us.

I heard about a little boy who was writing a letter to God, listing all the things he wanted for Christmas. Tongue between his teeth in concentration, the little guy penciled the words: "Dear God, I have been good for six months now." But then he thought about it for a moment, crossed out "six" and wrote in "three." He thought about it a little bit more, crossed out "three months," and wrote in "two weeks." After considering matters again, he looked over and noticed the manger scene his mother had set up on the coffee table. He walked over and picked up the little figurine of Mary, who was standing next to Joseph, came back to his letter, and continued, "Dear God, if You ever want to see Your mother again..."

Most of us have many expectations wrapped up in the giving and receiving of Christmas gifts in our culture. It's a big thing. We can get so psyched up about hoping we've found "the perfect gift" for someone. Or we dread that polite-but-disappointed expression people show on their faces sometimes. Or maybe (though we wouldn't admit it) we hope our subtle hints have paid off and someone gets us what we really want.

I think we need to take a step back and put things into perspective.

I've found that the most precious moments of the Christmas season don't always come with the "main events" of Christmas dinner or opening presents under the tree. Sometimes it's those "in-between" times that really bring us joy and deliver the truly lasting memories. I'm talking about those simple, relaxed moments when you're with family and friends and find yourself really savoring the friendship and love.

I heard a story about a very old woman who was losing her sight. She had three sons. When Christmas rolled around, each one wanted to show how much he loved his mother. The first son bought his mother a lovely fifteen-room mansion. The second son, not wanting to be outdone, signed papers on a brand new Rolls Royce, complete with a driver, hoping that it would win her approval. So what was Son Number Three to do? How could he top those gifts? After thinking about it for a while, he went out and bought his nearly blind mother a trained parrot.

What was so unusual about this parrot is it that it had spent fifteen years memorizing the entire Bible. You could go to this parrot, give it a Bible reference, and the parrot would quote it word for word. He paid a great deal of money for it, as there was only one in all the world. He thought that would be a wonderful gift for a lady who was losing her ability to see.

So the mother received all of the gifts from her sons on Christmas day.

She called up her first son and said, "Thank you so much for that beautiful mansion, but really, son—I only live in one room of my house as it is. A mansion would really be too much work for me, with so many rooms to keep clean. So thank you for your kindness, but I really have to give it back to you."

Calling up her second son, she said, "Son, thank you so much for that beautiful Rolls Royce. I loved it, and that was so thoughtful. But I didn't really like the driver all that much, and, to tell you the truth, I don't like to go out much any more. Bless you for the gift, but I'm returning it to you."

Then she called up her third son and said, "Son, thank you so much for that thoughtful gift. The chicken was small, but delicious!"

As the Christmas holidays draw near, I think it's important for each of us to discover or rediscover what the essential message of Christmas is really all about.

"GOD WITH US"

Here's how the Gospel writer Matthew picks up the account.

Now the birth of Jesus Christ was as follows: After His mother Mary was betrothed to Joseph, before they came together, she was found with child of the Holy Spirit. Then Joseph her husband, being a just man, and not wanting to make her a public example, was minded to put her away secretly. But while he thought about these things, behold, an angel of the Lord appeared to him in a dream, saying, "Joseph, son of David, do not be afraid to take to you Mary your wife, for that which is conceived in her is of the Holy Spirit. And she will bring forth a Son, and you shall call His name JESUS, for He will save His people from their sins."

So all this was done that it might be fulfilled which was spoken by the Lord through the prophet, saying: "Behold, the virgin shall be with child, and bear a Son, and they shall call His name Immanuel," which is translated, "God with us."

Then Joseph, being aroused from sleep, did as the angel of the Lord commanded him and took to him his wife, and did not know her till she had brought forth her firstborn Son. And he called His name JESUS. (Matthew 1:18-25)

The Bible says that Joseph was a righteous man and wanted to do the right thing. He had two basic options on the table. One was to publicly tell everyone what she had done, with the understanding that the young woman could be executed for such a serious sin. Or he could try to draw the curtains on this whole sad chapter, put her away privately, and quietly terminate the relationship. He chose the latter course. He would simply bear that heartache, step away from Mary's life, and that would be the end of it. Period.

Have you ever noticed how the Lord sometimes turns our periods into commas, and our commas into periods? From our human point of view, we see something going forward and continuing on, but God steps in and says, "No, that's over now." At other times we think something is over and done with, and God comes along and says, "You might think the vision is dead, but it isn't. I'm about to bring it to life again."

That's what He did in this case. Joseph had placed a firm period in his heart regarding his future with Mary, but the Lord slipped in and turned the period into a comma. There would be more to come... much more than Joseph could have ever dreamed. The angel told Joseph that this miracle child in Mary's womb would, in fact, be Israel's long-awaited Messiah. He dropped that bombshell in verse 21: "And she will bring forth a Son, and you shall call His name JESUS, for He will save His people from their sins."

To tell Joseph to name the child Jesus was one thing. A lot of young boys were called Jesus or Joshua or Yeshua in those days. It was a common name, much like John would be today. Did the angel quote the book of Isaiah to Joseph at that point? It looks like that's what he may have done.

So all this was done that it might be fulfilled which was spoken by the Lord through the prophet, saying: "Behold, the virgin shall be with child, and bear a Son, and they shall call His name Immanuel," which is translated, "God with us." (vv. 22-23)

The angel was saying, "Joseph, not only has Mary been faithful to you, contrary to what you thought, but she is to be the virgin spoken of by the prophet Isaiah."

That prophecy had been given seven hundred and fifty years before Joseph was born. It would be equivalent to a prophecy being made in AD 1257, then coming to pass today. And the prophecy would see its fulfillment in that sweet little teenager betrothed to Joseph. The child she was carrying was Immanuel, God With Us. What a staggering thought! And it's a truth that is the very essence of Christianity.

Here is a clear distinction between the Christian faith and all other world religions. Christianity is God with us. It's not us trying to somehow please or appease God, earn His approval, work our way into heaven, or reach a state of nirvana. The Christian faith teaches that God is with us, helping us to become the men and women He has called to be. Christianity says you will never be alone again.

God Himself will walk with you through life. Jesus echoed this same thought when He said, "Lo, I am with you always, even to the end of the age," and again, "I will never leave you nor forsake you."[44]

God... the Almighty... the Creator... the King of the Universe is with us! And not only with us, but in us. That is the astonishing message of Christmas. Every other depiction of Christmas pales before this radiant reality.

A MESSAGE TO REMEMBER

Could it be that you need to be reminded of this truth right now? Perhaps as you read these words you're feeling alone and lonely. You may be single, and you've never found that right man or woman to be your life partner. Maybe you never will. But God is with you. He will be your Life Partner!

Maybe your marriage is hanging by a thread right now. At this time of the year when so much emphasis is placed on family, you're experiencing severe and gut-wrenching marital problems. Even so, right in the heart of the storm, right in the middle of the heartache, God is with you!

Maybe you've become estranged from your children, with heartbreak and hard feelings in the mix. God is with you!

Maybe someone close to you has let you down or disappointed you. God is with you!

That is the message of Christmas that we must always remember.

Jesus took it even further when He said in Revelation 3:20, "Behold, I stand at the door and knock. If anyone hears My voice and opens the door, I will come in to him and dine with him, and he with Me." In other words,

"I'll have a meal with you!" But what does that mean? What do those words really imply?

In its original context, Jesus was addressing these words to the church of Laodicea. Laodicea was a church that had lost its love relationship with Jesus, replacing it with a cold, legalistic religion. In Revelation 3:20, Jesus was saying, "I want relationship. I want what we once had together." That's what is implied by the phrase, "I will dine with you."

In biblical times, eating a meal together was a very important activity. They didn't have the kind of fast-food restaurants we have today or lunch breaks that last for an hour or less. You know how it is; you have just enough time to run to your car, drive through McDonalds, gulp down your Big Mac, and get back to your desk. In biblical times they didn't drive their chariots through McDavid's. A meal was something that took time. Especially dinner. It was the main event of the day, and everyone looked forward to it.

It wasn't like the depiction we see in Leonardo DaVinci's "The Last Supper," where they are all seated in straight-backed chairs behind a really long table, with the Lord in the middle. It all looks pretty stiff, like they're posing for a photo. In New Testament times, they would sit around a table that was very low to the ground, and they wouldn't have chairs at all—they would be reclining on pillows. A meal could last for hours. In addition to fish, they would have various sauces on the table, and they would take pieces of unleavened bread and dip them into the sauce. It was a time of talking, listening, laughing, and discussing the events of the day. In other words, it was a very important time of intimacy and closeness.

So Jesus was saying to the Laodiceans—and to us—"I'm outside your door, knocking. If you hear My voice, open the door and I'll come in! We'll spend time together, like friends or family members around the table. We'll be intimate."

This is a mark of friendship, isn't it? When you want to go out and have a meal with someone, do you look for the first stranger on the street? Generally not. You want to go out to eat with someone you feel close to. If you're really close with them, you will even eat off of their plate. If you are really, really close, you won't even ask to eat off of their plate, you'll just take stuff!

When you have friends over and invite them into your home, where do you sit? If your best friend comes in, do you go into the living room? No. Where do you go? The kitchen! Recently my wife, Cathe, and I went to a party in a person's home. For the most part, everyone ended up in the kitchen. Why? Well, for one thing, the food was there in easy reach! But there's also something about a kitchen that's informal and relaxed. It's a great place to hang out and talk.

That's the idea here in this familiar passage of Scripture. Dining with the Lord speaks of closeness and intimacy. Jesus is saying, "This is what I desire with you. I want fellowship. I want friendship. I want closeness." God wants to come into your kitchen, sit at the counter, eat some chips and salsa, and hear what's really on your heart. Amazing! One of my favorite songs at this time of year goes,

O come, O come, Emmanuel
And ransom captive Israel.…

O come, Thou Wisdom from on high,
Who orderest all things mightily;
To us the path of knowledge show,
And teach us in her ways to go.

We sing, "O come, O come Immanuel," but do we really mean it? Do we really want Him to come? Even if it inconveniences us and changes our lives? Are we prepared for all that close fellowship with Him includes? Do we want Christmas all year long, or just one day on the calendar? Do we just want the Lord home for the holidays, or are we ready to invite Him in as a permanent resident?

God is with us. What does that mean? Let's go to another passage of Scripture to get a better understanding of that.

At Home and Settled In

The apostle Paul wrote a prayer for the believers in Ephesus, but it's really a heart cry for all true believers.

For this reason I bow my knees to the Father of our
Lord Jesus Christ, from whom the whole family in
heaven and earth is named, that He would grant you,
according to the riches of His glory, to be strengthened
with might through His Spirit in the inner man, that
Christ may dwell in your hearts through faith; that
you, being rooted and grounded in love, may be able
to comprehend with all the saints what is the width
and length and depth and height—to know the love
of Christ which passes knowledge; that you may be
filled with all the fullness of God. (Ephesians 3:14-19)

In verse 17, Paul prays that Christ would dwell in their hearts. Why would he pray that for a believer? Clearly the people he is addressing in Ephesus were already believers; in earlier chapters he points out the fact that they have been justified, sanctified, and adopted into God's family. So to a group of Christians—to men and women who already have a relationship with God through Christ—Paul is saying, "My prayer for you is that Christ may dwell in your hearts through faith."

What does that mean? A better understanding of the original language gives some insight into that question. The phrase "to dwell" could be translated "to live in a house." In the original language it could be translated this way: to settle down or be at home in a house. Paul is praying that Christ would settle down in their hearts—not just be inside the house of their hearts, so to speak, but be at home there... settled down as a family member.

Is Christ at home in your heart today? I didn't ask if He lives there. If you have put your faith in Jesus, He has already taken residence in you. He is in you. Scripture speaks of "Christ in you, the hope of glory."[45] That's not the issue. The question is, is He comfortable there? Is He settled down there? Is He at home there?

What does it mean when it speaks of Christ taking up residence in your heart? In our modern use of the word "heart," we tend to think of something that encompasses our emotions. We might say, "My mind tells me to do one thing, but my heart tells me to do another." By that we mean, "Intellectually I know this is what I ought to do, but down in my heart of hearts I really want to do this other thing instead."

We tend to think of the heart as the emotional aspect of our lives—our gut reactions. And so often we find our heart and our mind in conflict.

That wasn't the case in biblical times. In the language of the New Testament, heart referred to the mind. It spoke of the seat of understanding, as well as the will. It has been said, "The heart is a citadel of the soul." In Ephesians, Paul prays that Jesus Christ would settle down in your affections, in your emotions, that He would dwell in your will and be the dominating factor in the whole of life—controlling and directing it. Jesus Christ wants to live in the very center of your being.

I ask you again, is Jesus at home in your heart? Are you at home with Jesus? Or let me state it another way: Are you at home with godly people? It seems to me that if you are truly at home with Jesus and He is at home with you, you will find that you want to surround yourself with people who share those priorities. That would say to me that you are serious about your spiritual life. What kind of people do you hang around with? What kind of people do you engage with? If they are godly people, it would seem that Jesus is at home in your life. If they are ungodly people, what does that say?

You might say, "I have my Christian friends, and they're okay, but these are the friends I really like to be with. They don't know the Lord, but we have a lot of fun." Wait a second. I have found that my godly friends are the most fun to be around. Do you know why that is? It's because we have sanctified fun. We laugh. We have a good time.

We joke around. But then a conversation can turn serious in a matter of seconds, and someone will say, "Let's pray about that right now."

That is a completely natural spirituality, and I love it. Sometimes I think people don't understand that you can be a spiritual person and still have a full and happy life with lots of laughter.

Spiritual. . . and Loving It!

When I was a teenager and new to the faith, I used to think to myself, I can't be the person I used to be. I was a goof-off and a prankster in school, always joking around. After I became a believer, I kept telling myself, Greg, you're a Christian now. You have to be serious. No more joking around or pulling pranks. That would be unspiritual.

I remember the first time I went up to a Calvary Chapel summer camp, around the age of seventeen. One day at lunch, I happened to find myself sitting at a table with Chuck Smith, the pastor. How am I supposed to act around such a man of God? I asked myself. I remember feeling a little nervous and tense.

After downing a glass of punch, I was still thirsty and wanted some more. But that would mean asking Pastor Chuck to pass me the pitcher.

Finally I worked up my courage and said, "Um, Pastor Chuck, I was wondering. Could I get a little more punch?"

"Sure!" he said. He took the pitcher of punch and began filling my glass—and filling and filling it! He filled it up to the top, and then it started to overflow and pour down my arm. I looked up and saw that he was laughing. Wait a second!

Was Pastor Chuck joking around with me? Does this mean I can be a Christian and still goof off?

Yes, that's exactly what it meant.

Anyone who knows me can tell you that I have plenty of fun. And that's the way it should be! I think a group of Christian friends who love Jesus can enjoy each other and have more fun than anyone else. You trust each other. You're relaxed around each other. You know what matters in life, and you've been freed from much of the cynicism, mask-wearing, game-playing, and one-upmanship that characterized your lives before Christ.

Jesus liked to spend time with all kinds of people. But just as it was in His day, some people think it's "not spiritual" to really enjoy yourself and have a great time. If they had it their way, while everyone else in the room was talking and laughing, they'd be over in the corner reading their Bible.

Am I making light of Bible reading? Of course not. I'm simply saying that there's a time to read the Bible and there's a time to go out and live the Bible—to be an attractive, winsome, friendly person whom other people like to be around.

SOMEONE'S KNOCKING

Let's play this out now. Let's say you've just gotten home from church. You've changed into your comfortable clothes, have a new flick playing on your DVD player, and are getting ready for lunch.

There's a knock on the door. Of all people, it's Billy Graham. "Dr. Graham," you say, more than a little surprised. "Why are you here?"

"I just wanted to come into your home for a visit," he replies in that unmistakable southern accent.

"Well. . . um, that's wonderful. Please do come in."

The great evangelist steps inside and starts walking through your home. The movie is playing away in the family room, and the kids are acting like usually do. All of a sudden you become very self-conscious. *What DVD is playing?* you ask yourself. Oh no, I don't want Billy Graham to see that! He glances at the magazine you have open on the kitchen counter, and you're embarrassed. Why did I leave that thing lying there? What's he going to think? Suddenly you become aware of what's going on in your home, because a man of God has walked through the front door.

Now let's switch the analogy. It's isn't Billy Graham, it's the Lord Jesus Himself. You've opened the door, He has stepped inside, and now He's taking a little walk through your life, looking at everything. You sang, "O come, O come Immanuel," and He really did!

By the way, He's not interested in coming into your life for a short visit; He plans on staying. He's moving in, and He has no intention of living in a corner of your little guest room. He's taking the whole place over. Are you ready for that? Isn't that what you prayed for?

Maybe you've seen that classical little book called "My Heart, Christ's Home," written by Robert Boyd Monger and published by Intervarsity Press. As clearly as anyone has ever done it, Monger takes this concept of our heart being like a home and makes it come alive in story form.

He writes of Jesus coming to His home and desiring to walk around—and uses the various rooms of a house as a metaphor for the human heart.

In the booklet, Monger speaks of the first room that he and Jesus enter together.

The first room was the study—the library. In my home this room of the mind is a very small room with very thick walls. But it is a very important room. In a sense, it is the control room of the house. He entered with me and looked around at the books in the bookcase, the magazines upon the table, the pictures on the walls.

As I followed His gaze I became uncomfortable. Strangely, I had not felt self-conscious about this before, but now that He was there looking at these things I was embarrassed. Some books were there that His eyes were too pure to behold. On the table were a few magazines that a Christian had no business reading. As for the pictures on the walls—the imaginations and thoughts of the mind—some of these were shameful.

Red-faced, I turned to Him and said, "Master, I know that this room needs to be cleaned up and made over. Will You help me make it what it ought to be?"

"Certainly!" He said, "I'm glad to help you. First of all, take all the things that you are reading and looking at which are not helpful, pure, good and true, and throw them out! Now put on the empty shelves the books of the Bible. Fill the library with Scripture and meditate

on it day and night. As for the pictures on the walls,
you will have difficulty controlling these images, but I
have something that will help." He gave me a full-sized
portrait of Himself. "Hang this centrally," He said, "on
the wall of the mind."

I did, and I have discovered through the years that
when my thoughts are centered upon Christ Himself,
His purity and power cause impure thoughts to back
away. So He has helped me to bring my thoughts under
His control.

Imagine that Jesus is in your home. He sits down at your computer, and you notice that He's going to your Web browser to check out your bookmarks. Do you have any problem with that? Or do you find yourself saying, "Oh Lord, please don't mess with the computer." If He were to go back over the Web sites you've visited in the last week or two, would there be some things that would embarrass you? Would you be concerned about what you've been watching on TV or what movies you've rented?

If so, then I wonder if He is really at home in your life.

Have you ever walked into a home and for whatever reason, you felt immediately uncomfortable and just wanted to leave? You didn't want to take your coat off, did you? You just wanted an excuse to back right out of there and go somewhere else. You thought to yourself, Let's get this over with. I'm not at home here. This place creeps me out.

I wonder if Jesus would feel that way in some of our hearts. He is there, He is a resident, but He's not at home.

He's not comfortable. He doesn't want to walk into your kitch-en. He doesn't want to hang out because of all of this junk you have in your life. Maybe as He walks around your home He says, "I smell something strange. Do you smell that?"

"Well, no," you say, "I don't smell anything."

He follows the smell and locates the offending odor behind a certain door.

"That's just my closet, Lord," you say.

"What do you have in there?"

"Well, some skeletons, I guess."

"Why don't we roll up our sleeves and clean it out together?"

"Lord, trust me, you don't want to open that door."

"Yes, I do. I already know what's back there. I think we need to clean it out. Just let me have a go at it."

"Lord, I'd just rather that You didn't."

"You asked me to come and live in your home, right?"

"Well, yes, I did."

"You asked me to be Lord of all, right?"

"Yes, I did."

"Then I want to open up this closet and clean it out. It's toxic. It's poison. It's affecting everything else."

"I would rather You didn't."

"I need the key right now."

You reluctantly place it in His hand.

"All right."

He opens up that closet. You turn away. You don't even want to see what He's about to see. To your amazement, He dives in and starts pulling things out. He gets out the brush and soap and disinfectant. He's down on His hands and knees, bringing order to your life, getting rid of that

filth and junk that has plagued you for so long. And not
only that, He's bringing in new things to replace the old,
rotten stuff. You're discovering that the only reason He
wanted to get rid of the old garbage was to put something
far better in its place.

"O come, O come, Immanuel."

Are you ready to sing that and mean it?

HAND HIM THE KEYS

Back in the book of Ephesians, Paul writes these moving
words:

> *In those days you were living apart from Christ. You
> were excluded from citizenship among the people Is-
> rael, and you did not know the covenant promises God
> had made to them. You lived in this world without God
> and without hope. But now you have been united with
> Christ Jesus. Once you were far away from God, but
> now you have been brought near to him through the
> blood of Christ. (Ephesians 2:12-13, NLT)*

There was a time in our lives when we did not have Immanuel. God was not with us. Jesus was not in our lives.
At that time we were without God and without hope.

We have a choice before us right now. We can be without God and without hope, or we can have God with us.
Christmas will soon be over. You'll wrap the Christmas
lights up into a big ball that will take you hours to undo
next year. The pretty wrapping paper will be wadded up
and headed for a landfill. Those new toys you couldn't wait

to play with will break or lose their attraction, and the season will be past.

Depressing? If you have Immanuel in your life, who cares? That's all that matters.

I will tell you very honestly, if I didn't have Christ living in me, I wouldn't have any hope right now. And as you look at this world and the state it's in, and how we always live on the razor edge of crisis and disaster, there isn't much to give any reason for optimism or joy. But when Immanuel enters the picture, everything changes.

Open the door and let Him in. And then hand Him the keys to the house—all of them—and let Him be at home.

FIVE

Come, Let Us Adore Him

This is a story about true and false worshipers. Interestingly, those who should have known the most about worship—the chief priests and scribes and even King Herod himself—knew the least. And those that should have known the least about worship—pagan Wise Men from the East—knew the most. But in them we will see worship as it ought to be.

You might say, "When you say 'worship,' do you mean the songs people sing in church? I'm not really interested in a topic like that."

Yes, worship certainly includes singing. But it's much more than that.

My youngest son, Jonathan, once asked me, "Dad, why did God put us here on the earth?"

"Do you really want to know the answer to that?" I asked him.

"Yes," he said. "I want to know."

"Jonathan," I said, "God put us here on the earth so that we might worship Him and glorify Him and know the God who created us."

In other words, man's ultimate purpose in life is not to attain success or fame or even happiness. Rather, man's ultimate purpose in life is to know the God who made him.

And until we enter into that relationship, we fall short of what is possible and attainable to us.

In fact, Scripture says in the book of Revelation that those in heaven sing, "You are worthy, O Lord our God, to receive glory and honor and power. For you created all things, and they exist because you created what you pleased."[46]

You and I were created to worship God and bring pleasure to Him. And when we get down to it, everybody does worship. Now certainly we don't all worship the true God in heaven. But everyone, no matter who they are, worships someone or something. Human beings are hardwired for that, and really can't get away from it.

Some people worship people they know.

Some worship celebrities—sports heroes or actors or musicians.

Some worship possessions.

Some people worship themselves.

But when you get down to it, every person everywhere worships. Atheists... agnostics... infidels... skeptics... Republicans... Democrats... Independents, worship!

But what do they worship? That all depends. Some worship a god of their own making, while others worship the true and living God. But everyone worships something. The Bible says that God has placed eternity in the heart of man.[47] That is simply how we were created—with the sense that there's something more to life than what we experience on this earth.

There are many—even in Christian circles—who teach that humans evolved from the animal kingdom.

But if the Bible is true (and it is), then that theory cannot be true. Scripture clearly teaches that God uniquely created man in His own image. He did not create animals in that way.

I have had many dogs over the years, and I don't know one of them who would sit in the backyard having a worship experience with the Lord. I know they never laid out there in the sun thinking about the love and holiness of God or the wonder of eternity. My dogs basically sat there and had thoughts like, I want to eat now. And after that I want to lay in the sun and take a nap. Then I want to eat again. Something along those lines, I'm sure. God has only placed eternity—that longing for something or someone beyond ourselves—in the hearts of men and women. And that is what causes people everywhere to worship.

Many people, of course, worship gods of their own making and out of their own imagination. Sometimes you will hear people say, "Let me tell you something. My god would never condemn a person to hell. I don't believe in a god that would ever bring a penalty for sin. My god is all-loving and caring. My god is this and that… blah, blah, blah."

Let me just say to those who say these things that your god doesn't exist anywhere except in the realm of your imagination. Because when you speak like that, you are not speaking of the true and living God, you are speaking of your own little cobbled-together-god—with a small "g"—that you have created in your own image. But the God of the Bible—the one-and-only God—is the one who deserves our worship and devotion. A god of our making will ultimately disappoint us.

So let's learn a bit about what worship should be, and let's learn it from the Christmas story itself,

TRUE SEEKERS

Now after Jesus was born in Bethlehem of Judea in the days of Herod the king, behold, Wise Men from the East came to Jerusalem, saying, "Where is He who has been born King of the Jews? For we have seen His star in the East and have come to worship Him."

When Herod the king heard this, he was troubled, and all Jerusalem with him. And when he had gathered all the chief priests and scribes of the people together, he inquired of them where the Christ was to be born.

So they said to him, "In Bethlehem of Judea, for thus it is written by the prophet: 'But you, Bethlehem, in the land of Judah, are not the least among the rulers of Judah; for out of you shall come a Ruler Who will shepherd My people Israel.'"

Then Herod, when he had secretly called the Wise Men, determined from them what time the star appeared. And he sent them to Bethlehem and said, "Go and search carefully for the young Child, and when you have found Him, bring back word to me, that I may come and worship Him also."

When they heard the king, they departed; and behold, the star which they had seen in the East went before them, till it came and stood over where the young Child was.

When they saw the star, they rejoiced with exceedingly
great joy. And when they had come into the house, they
saw the young Child with Mary His mother, and fell
down and worshiped Him. And when they had opened
their treasures, they presented gifts to Him: gold,
frankincense, and myrrh.

Then, being divinely warned in a dream that they
should not return to Herod, they departed for their
own country another way.

Now when they had departed, behold, an angel of
the Lord appeared to Joseph in a dream, saying,
"Arise, take the young Child and His mother, flee
to Egypt, and stay there until I bring you word; for
Herod will seek the young Child to destroy Him."

When he arose, he took the young Child and His mother
by night and departed for Egypt, and was there until
the death of Herod, that it might be fulfilled which was
spoken by the Lord through the prophet, saying, "Out
of Egypt I called My Son." (Matthew 2:1-15)

We spoke briefly a little earlier about these Magi, or
Wise Men. These men who were schooled not only in
astronomy, but astrology, did not find the answers they
were looking for in life in their occultic practices. But it
is apparent that they were seeking the truth. You might
say there were true seekers. Why do I say that? Because
God actually revealed Himself to them in a special way.

God says in Jeremiah 29:13-14 (NIV), "You will seek me and find me when you seek me with all of your heart. I will be found by you."

Many in today's world are trapped in false religious systems or cults. But I believe that if a man or woman truly desires to know the true God, and seeks after Him with all their heart, He will reveal Himself to them and deliver them from error.

That, I believe, was the case with these Magi from the East. Look how God came to these men. To what did these men most closely relate? They related to the stars. They looked to the stars to chart their course. And how did God come to them? He brought a star. To lead them where? To the real Messiah.

ON OUR LEVEL

I am always amazed to hear the personal testimonies of people who have come to Jesus Christ—often out of the most unbelievable backgrounds and circumstances. To hear the story of men and women in seemingly hopeless situations: strung out on drugs. . . hooked on alcohol. . . addicted to pornography. . . and how the Lord reached down to pluck them out of that quicksand, saved them, and gave them a new life. Or I think of someone like Christopher Parkening, a guitar virtuoso at the top of his field. He had realized all of the dreams and aspirations that he had in life—including a personal trout farm on his ranch in Montana. But God came to him and showed him a gaping emptiness in his soul. And Christopher gave His life to Christ. God will come to each person on a level they can understand.

I don't care what their background is, their age, race, or culture. Jesus Christ can reach all of us.

Because He loved the Magi, God sent them a star to bring them to Himself. Now these fellows had followed the star across hundreds of miles. But apparently they took their eyes off of it, because if they had followed it carefully, it would have led them to Bethlehem. But instead they ended up in Jerusalem. Probably what happened is they saw the star in that general area, and of course Bethlehem is not that not far from Jerusalem, so they assumed the star would be leading them to Jerusalem—the spiritual capital of the world.

We read about them coming into Jerusalem saying, "Where is He that is born the King of the Jews? We have seen His star in the East and we have come to worship Him." But instead of finding the King they were looking for, they encountered a paranoid puppet king known as Herod, who wanted to manipulate them for his own ends. Herod was the king of Jerusalem, a cruel despot who ruled with an iron fist.

In fact, Jerusalem would later receive their King. They would later receive Jesus by sending Him outside of the city to be crucified. His crown would be one made of thorns instead of one imbedded with diamonds and fine jewels. His throne would be a cross of wood instead of a regal throne of gold. That's how they would recognize their king.

But as these dignitaries from the East arrived in Jerusalem, they said, "We have come to worship this King of the Jews." Here are these pagan astrologers who seem to have—at least at this moment, with as little light as they had received—a better understanding of what worship was and is than Herod or even the Bible scholars he summoned later, saying, "Tell me where the Messiah is ultimately to be born."

Now the word the Wise Men used for "worship" here is important. It comes from an old English word that means "worth-ship." It means to worship something because it merits your worship and is worthy of praise and adulation.

So when I come together with other believers on Sunday morning and the leader opens the service with song, saying, "Let's worship the Lord," why should I? Because "I feel like it" and I'm in a really good mood? What if I'm not in a good mood at all? Does that mean I should slouch in my chair and just skip the worship? No. I should worship because God is worthy. And no matter what I may be going through at the moment, no matter what the circumstances are in my life, God merits my worship.

The psalmist cried out:

Praise the Lord!
Oh, give thanks to the Lord, for He is good!
For His mercy endures forever.
(Psalm 106:1)

So I worship God in spite of my circumstances, in spite of what I have endured or am enduring. Why? Because God is good, and He always merits and deserves my worship. That is why we should all engage when we worship together. It's not appropriate for some of us to say, "I don't really want to worship." We were created to worship God.

So who am I—or who are you—to fold our arms and say, "I'm not going to worship tonight"? God made us to worship Him. God made us to bring Him pleasure. And God is most pleased when we worship Him from a proper heart. It's something we are commanded to do.

FAITH OVER CIRCUMSTANCES

I'll tell you a little secret here. Sometimes when you worship the Lord your problems won't go away. But they won't seem as significant, either. And it's not because your problems have disappeared, but it's because you reevaluated things. You've gotten some perspective.

Sometimes when you walk into church the awareness of your problems is a mile high, and your awareness of God is an inch high. But then you begin to worship—really worship in the Spirit and in truth. You honor and praise Him for His glory, power, splendor, love, and faithfulness. And when you walk out of church, your problems and God have exchanged positions. Your problems are an inch high, and He is a mile high in your heart, towering over everything. Life is back in its true perspective.

It's all in how you look at things. If you have a big God, then you will have small problems. If you have a small god, then you will have big problems. The choice is yours.

I'm not talking about positive thinking, positive confession, or "mind over matter" here. I'm talking about faith over circumstances. I am simply talking about honoring the true God who is still on the throne no matter what you may be facing.

He may deliver you immediately from your situation. That's what He chose to do with Paul and Silas in that filthy dungeon in Philippi. As they sang, an earthquake rumbled through town and the whole prison fell apart. Talk about bringing the house down! It was their first European concert.

Remember, however, that at other times God chose not to deliver Paul from prison, persecution, heartache, and eventually his execution. But even in prison, possibly looking toward his date with the executioner, Paul wrote: "Rejoice in the Lord always. Again I will say, rejoice!"[48] Sometimes God will change your circumstances. Sometimes He won't. But He is always worthy of your worship.

The phrase the Wise Men used, "We have come to worship Him," is a phrase that could be translated, "We have come to bow down before Him and do homage." What an amazing statement to come from these high-ranking dignitaries from a distant land. They came to King Herod and said, "We want to worship the true and living God. We're ready to bow ourselves down and lay prostrate before His majesty."

Now another word that is used in the Bible for worship could be translated "to kiss toward." And that idea speaks of affection. When you put these two concepts together, you get a well-rounded idea of what worship should be. On one hand, it is reverent and honoring. I stand in awe of a holy and flawless God. But on the other hand, this God who is holy and flawless sent His Son to die on the cross for me. He made a new and living way for me to know Him in a personal way, and I can enter into friendship with Him. So I can "kiss toward Him," so to speak. I can have affection.

As you might imagine, it's easy for us to get out of balance and tip too far one way or another in our worship. There are those who say, "I'm afraid of God. If I slip up, He's going to nail me. I'm not sure I can ever please Him." Then, on the other side, there are those who are overly casual—almost flippant—about their worship. We need to find the right balance between the reverence and honor of a holy God and our close, affectionate, personal relationship with Him.

And that's exactly what worship should be.

GIFTS OF WORSHIP

The Magi, whose hearts were set on worship, brought gifts to the young King—very unusual gifts to present to a child, as we have said. These gifts, however, were but an extension, or overflow, of hearts that were filled with worship. Right worship must be the only basis for right giving and right service. Why do I do these things? Why do I give gifts to the Lord? Why do I give Him my time, talent, and treasures? I do it out of the fullness of my heart, because I love Him.

Some people come to church with great expectations, looking for "something profound" to happen in the service. If their expectations aren't met, they will say, "I didn't get anything out of church Sunday. It was boring. . . . I don't think that I like that church anymore. Their worship doesn't move me."

Hold on now. Did you ever stop and think that the problem might be with you, rather than the church? If you have gone Monday through Saturday without worshiping God, you can't expect Sunday morning to be a profound experience of closeness with the Lord. Your heart hasn't been prepared! Sunday worship should be the overflow of a week of walking with God and enjoying His presence. The worship in the sanctuary is largely meaningless unless it is preceded by and prepared for by the worship of life. Living a life of worship means that I seek to glorify God in all I say and do.

"Well," you say, "I'm not particularly musical, and I don't speak well. How am I supposed to bring God glory?" That's fine. But what can you do? Can you program a computer? Can you frame a house? Can you create a wonderful meal? Can you employ some artistic ability or write a poem or repair a car or care for a young child? Great! Take whatever you have, whatever God has gifted you to do, and use it for His glory. God can use you in whatever vocation you're in. Whatever you do, you can do it to the best of your ability—with a smile and a sweet attitude—and become an effective witness for Jesus.

A FALSE WORSHIPER

Just as these Wise Men were true worshipers, there is a false worshiper in our story. And of course it was Herod. Who was this guy that we call Herod? At the tender age of twenty-five, he was named governor of Galilee, a very prestigious position for such a young man. The Romans were hoping he could somehow get control of the Jews living in that area. So in 40 BC, the Roman senate had Herod named "the king of the Jews." It was a title he loved, and it was a title the Hebrews hated because he was anything but religious... and wasn't even a Jew!

King Herod was a shrewd and brutal tyrant. He was also paranoid. At times (for political advantage) he could be perceived as benevolent and kind. On one occasion, in a time of economic hardship, he gave back tax money to the people that had been collected for the Temple. They appreciated that. On another occasion, during a famine in 25 BC, he melted down various gold objects in the palace to buy food for the poor. As a result, he definitely had his supporters in Jerusalem.

He was also a great visionary and builder. You can go to Israel today, some 2000 years after Herod lived and died, and still see the remains of his incredible structures. Compare that with our buildings today! If there is a building still standing from the 1920's, we're amazed.

Herod was responsible for rebuilding the second Temple. Solomon built the first one, which was ultimately destroyed in the Babylonian invasion. Herod took the modest second Temple, rebuilt under Ezra, and spent forty-seven years remodeling and refurbishing it. Talk about a long building project. But it was a beautiful, magnificent structure.

Herod also had a magnificent palace—and even a winter hideaway where he could go in the cold months of the year, a place called Masada. I have personally visited that mountaintop fortress. Do you realize that 2000 years ago Herod put in a swimming pool and a sauna at his winter digs? This guy knew how to build!

But you see, Masada was also built as a fortress, because he was always paranoid that someone was going to appear on the scene and try to take away his kingdom. So if there was one thing you did not want to say to Herod, it was,

"Where is He that is born the king of the Jews?" Rome had given that very title to Herod! Imagine the dialogue with these foreign dignitaries.

"Where is the king of the Jews?"

"You're looking at him, boys."

"No, you're not the one we're looking for. The star didn't lead us here. We're still searching."

"What? I'm not the king? There's another one somewhere?"

That really pushed Herod's button. Suddenly he realized there was another king in town. What did that mean? In the mind of a paranoid tyrant like Herod, it meant search and destroy. Anyone who was a competitor to Herod would die. In fact, history tells us that he had his own three sons and his wife executed because he imagined them to be a threat to his kingdom. That's what gave rise to the saying bandied about in that day: "Better to be one of Herod's pigs than his sons." If you crossed Herod, if you bothered him, if he saw you as a threat, you were history.

A CRUEL MASQUERADE

Small wonder Herod was troubled by the tidings from the Wise Men! The word translated "troubled" in Matthew 2:3 could also be rendered agitated or disturbed. He was all shook up! That's when he gave his terrible decree that all the male children in his kingdom two years old or younger should be put to death. Herod became the Butcher of Bethlehem. Josephus the historian called him barbaric. He didn't want anyone to be king except him.

Before the slaughter of the innocents took place, however, Herod gave instructions to the Magi:

"Go and search carefully for the young Child, and when you have found Him, bring back word to me, that I may come and worship Him also" (v. 8). Liar! He didn't want to worship this young Messiah. Worship was the last thing on his mind. He wanted to kill him.

Just as the Wise Men were true worshipers, Herod was a false one. He was hostile to God. He wanted to destroy, uproot, and oppose the plan of God. Yet in the process, he masqueraded as a worshiper of God.

Herods by the dozens, maybe even the thousands, sit in the pews of many churches today. Outwardly they appear devout and deeply religious, but they are living a lie. They don't know God. They don't have a relationship with Him. They may lift their hands and sing the songs, they may even drop money in the offering plate, say, "Praise the Lord," and do all the right and expected things. But that doesn't mean they are true worshipers. God looks on the heart.

The fact is, God would rather have no worship at all than phony worship. In the book of Malachi, God was so nauseated by the false worship and the sneering, whining attitude of the priests of that day that He said, "Why doesn't one of you just shut the Temple doors and lock them? Then none of you can get in and play at religion with this silly, empty-headed worship. I am not pleased. . . . And I don't want any more of this so-called worship!"[49]

If you have any doubt at all that God despises phony, insincere worship, read these startling words from the book of Isaiah:

*"What makes you think I want all your sacrifices?"
says the Lord. "I am sick of your burnt offerings of
rams and the fat of fattened cattle. I get no pleasure
from the blood of bulls and lambs and goats. When you
come to worship me, who asked you to parade through
my courts with all your ceremony? Stop bringing me
your meaningless gifts; the incense of your offerings
disgusts me! As for your celebrations of the new moon
and the Sabbath and your special days for fasting—
they are all sinful and false. I want no more of your
pious meetings. I hate your new moon celebrations
and your annual festivals. They are a burden to me.
I cannot stand them! When you lift up your hands in
prayer, I will not look. Though you offer many prayers,
I will not listen, for your hands are covered with the
blood of innocent victims."[50]*

If your life isn't right with God when you come into
church and sing and go through all of the rest of it, not
only does it not please Him, it is offensive to Him. You
can get away with that for a while, and even do a lot of
damage to innocent people, as Herod-the-baby-killer
did. But sooner or later, the day of reckoning comes.

In Matthew 2:19, the Scripture simply tells us that
Herod died. The wily old king may have conspired against
his enemies—and even his friends and family—to stay
in power. But he had no power at all against death, the
final enemy, and he had to appear before his Maker just
like everyone else will.

Jesus made it clear that there is a right and a wrong way to worship. He spoke of the Pharisees, who should have been experts at worship but by and large weren't even close. He said, "These people draw near to Me with their mouth, and honor Me with their lips, but their heart is far from Me. And in vain they worship Me."[51]

In other words, you can maintain external standards of worship—sing the songs, raise your hands, close your eyes—but if it's all show, if your heart isn't in it, God can't receive that worship. It doesn't do anything for anybody.

———— >●<‑ ————

True worship affects every aspect of our lives—and it's a lot more than showing up in church, making music, or going through the motions. The heart of authentic worship is living our lives in a way that is pleasing to God. Our singing and public prayer are but the outward manifestations of a life lived daily for the glory of God.

If that's what Christmas means to you... gratitude, heartfelt praise, and the open-handed yielding of your life to Immanuel, then December 25 will never disappoint you, never let you down. Others may not experience God's Christmas presence, but you will. And you'll find it fresh and new every year of your life.

ENDNOTES

1   Luke 2:46
2   Luke 2:49
3   C.S. Lewis, *The Problem of Pain*
4   Romans 6:23, NLT
5   2 Corinthians 9:15
6   Revelation 2:2-5, NIV
7   Luke 18:1
8   TLB, italics mine
9   See Luke 15:11-32
10 Mark 7:6-7, NIV
11 Luke 1:3-4, NLT
12 KJV
13 Philippians 2:6-7, NLT
14 Psalm 10:4, NIV
15 John 7:53-8:1
16 Luke 9:58
17 Isaiah 53:3, NIV
18 Luke 2:10
19 accessed at http://www.raystedman.org/misc/3018.html
20 NLT
21 Acts 16:25
22 C.S. Lewis, *Mere Christianity*
    (New York: Machillan Publishing Co., 1975) p.53-54.
23 John 1:3, NLT
24 Job 38:4-7, NLT
25 Isaiah 6:5, TLB
26 Jeremiah 1:6, NIV
27 Philippians 3:12-14, NLT

28 Revelation 3:17, NIV

29 Proverbs 9:17, TLB

30 Psalm 84:11

31 William Shakespeare, *Romeo and Juliet* (II, ii, 1-2)

32 John 3:16

33 Philippians 4:13

34 Philippians 4:7, TLB

35 James 1:5

36 2 Timothy 3:16-17, NLT

37 Philippians 2:12-13, *New King James Version*, and *The New Testament in Modern English*, by J. B. Phillips

38 Luke 2:14, NASB

39 Philippians 4:6-7, NLT

40 1 Corinthians 15:19, NLT

41 John 10:10, THE MESSAGE

42 John 15:13

43 John 4:10

44 Matthew 28:20; Hebrews 13:5

45 Colossians 1:27

46 Revelation 4:11, NLT

47 See Ecclesiastes 3:11.

48 Philippians 4:4

49 Malachi 1:10, THE MESSAGE

50 Isaiah 1:11-15, NLT

51 Matthew 15:8-9

About the Author

Greg Laurie is the pastor of Harvest Christian Fellowship (one of America's largest churches) in Riverside, California. He is the author of over thirty books, including the Gold Medallion Award winner, *The Upside-Down Church*, as well as *Every Day with Jesus; Are We Living in the Last Days?; Marriage Connections; Losers and Winners, Saints and Sinners;* and *Dealing with Giants.* You can find his study notes in the *New Believer's Bible* and the *Seeker's Bible.* Host of the *Harvest: Greg Laurie* television program and the nationally syndicated radio program, *A New Beginning*, Greg Laurie is also the founder and featured speaker for Harvest Crusades—contemporary, large-scale evangelistic outreaches, which local churches organize nationally and internationally. He and his wife, Cathe, live in Southern California and have two children and one grandchild.

Other AllenDavid books
Published by Kerygma
Publishing

Visit: www.kerygmapublishing.com
www.allendavidbooks.com
www.harvest.org